Financial Fitness for Life

Bringing Home the Gold
Grades 9-12

Student Workouts

John S. Morton
Mark C. Schug

NCEE

National Council on Economic Education

Authors:

John S. Morton is Vice President for Program Development at the National Council on Economic Education. Previously, he was a classroom teacher for 30 years and served as President of the Arizona Council on Economic Education. He has written numerous articles and publications in economic education.

Mark C. Schug is Director of the Center for Economic Education and Professor of Curriculum and Instruction at the University of Wisconsin-Milwaukee. He has taught for over 30 years at the middle school, high school, and university levels and has written widely in economic education.

Project Director:

John E. Clow is the Director of the Leatherstocking Center for Economic Education at the State University of New York, College at Oneonta and Professor Emeritus of that college. He is a national award-winning college teacher, speaker, and author in the fields of personal finance, economics, and business education.

Design:

Roher/Sprague Partners

This publication was made possible through funding by the Bank of America Foundation.

ISBN 1-56183-547-1

5 4 3

TABLE OF CONTENTS

9-12

THEME 3:

Tomorrow's Money: Getting to the End of the Rainbow
(Saving)

THEME 4:

Spending and Credit Are Serious Business
(Spending and Using Credit)

THEME 5:
Get a Plan: Get a Grip on Life
(Money Management)

THEME

1

There Is No Such Thing as a Free Lunch

OVERVIEW

You probably don't know much about managing your money. And what you don't know could hurt you. All your life you will be spending, borrowing, saving, and investing. You will be making economic decisions as a consumer, a worker, an investor, and a citizen. You will make choices today that will have major consequences for your future.

"What occupation should I pursue?" "Should I go to college?" "Should I get a credit card?" "Are all credit cards alike?" "Should I start saving now or wait until I have more of what I need?" "Should I invest in the stock market?" "What stocks or mutual funds should I invest in?"

The evidence is that most of you are not ready to make these choices. The average score on a recent national test on personal finance given to 12th graders was 51.9 percent. That's an "F" in any class. High school students received an even lower "F" on a national test about economics. The average score was only 48 percent. Your parents didn't do much better. Adults scored 57 percent on that same economics test. At least, they almost passed.

By now you may be thinking, "So what? Get off my case. How will understanding economics and personal finance help me? It's just more stuff people want me to learn in high school."

2

For openers, this information might make you rich. Achieving personal wealth involves planning and making sound financial choices, such as getting an education, saving early and often, comparison shopping, developing a money-management plan, and shopping for the best loan. You might be surprised to know that most millionaires in this country did not get rich quick by winning the lottery or inheriting money from a relative. They became rich by making sound choices, including these:

• Getting a good education.

• Working long, hard, and smart.

• Learning money-management skills.

• Living below their means.

• Investing in the stock market for the long term.

• Gathering information, developing criteria, and considering the alternatives before making decisions.

Learning to make smart choices is not rocket science. It might take some work, but you can learn this stuff. Your efforts now can have a big payoff later. How about starting on your first million bucks right now?

Questions

1. How much do high school students know about personal finance and economics?

2. What is personal finance?

3. Is there a payoff for learning personal finance?

ABOUT THERE IS NO SUCH THING AS A FREE LUNCH

1. What is an FAQ? *A Frequently Asked Question!*

2. Why is there no such thing as a free lunch?
Because of scarcity, we can't have everything we want—whether it's clothes, cars, or lunches. Every time we choose something, we have to give up something else. In other words, everything has a cost.

3. Why do some people have more money than others?
They have made wiser decisions regarding education, money management, and lifestyle.

4. How will studying personal finance improve my life?
This information will help you make better choices; better choices can lead to greater wealth and a more satisfying life.

5. What is an economic way of thinking?
A reasoning process that involves considering costs as well as benefits in making decisions.

6. Why do we have to make so many decisions?
Because of scarcity, we can't have everything we want.

7. Are things getting better or worse in the United States?
Things are definitely getting better. Here are a few examples. In 1970, the average size of a new home was 1,500 square feet, and by the late 1990s, the average size was 2,150 square feet. Only 34 percent of new homes had central heat and air conditioning in 1970, while 81 percent of new homes were so equipped in the late 1990s. In 1970, 20 percent of households had no car, and only 29 percent had two or more. By the late 1990s, only eight percent of households had no car, and 62 percent had two or more. The average net worth of a household in 1970 was $27,938, and in the late 1990s it was $59,398. You will probably live better than your parents as long as you get a good education and make sound financial decisions. Go for it!

The Millionaire Game Score Sheet

1. **True or False** **Score** **(-5 or +5)**
   (circle one)   (Millionaire card -10 or +10) ____

2. **True or False** **Score** **(-5 or +5)**
   (circle one)   (Millionaire card -10 or +10) ____

3. **True or False** **Score** **(-5 or +5)**
   (circle one)   (Millionaire card -10 or +10) ____

4. **True or False** **Score** **(-5 or +5)**
   (circle one)   (Millionaire card -10 or +10) ____

5. **True or False** **Score** **(-5 or +5)**
   (circle one)   (Millionaire card -10 or +10) ____

6. **True or False** **Score** **(-5 or +5)**
   (circle one)   (Millionaire card -10 or +10) ____

7. **True or False** **Score** **(-5 or +5)**
   (circle one)   (Millionaire card -10 or +10) ____

8. **True or False** **Score** **(-5 or +5)**
   (circle one)   (Millionaire card -10 or +10) ____

9. **True or False** **Score** **(-5 or +5)**
   (circle one)   (Millionaire card -10 or +10) ____

10. **True or False** **Score** **(-5 or +5)**
    (circle one)   (Millionaire card -10 or +10) ____

11. **True or False** **Score** **(-5 or +5)**
    (circle one)   (Millionaire card -10 or +10) ____

12. **True or False** **Score** **(-5 or +5)**
    (circle one)   (Millionaire card -10 or +10) ____

13. **True or False** **Score** **(-5 or +5)**
    (circle one)   (Millionaire card -10 or +10) ____

14. **True or False** **Score** **(-5 or +5)**
    (circle one)   (Millionaire card -10 or +10) ____

15. **True or False** **Score** **(-5 or +5)**
    (circle one)   (Millionaire card -10 or +10) ____

A Mystery of Two Families

The Robinsons and the Meltons are two families that earn the same income, live in the same neighborhood, are of the same age, and have two children each. Yet the Robinsons are six times wealthier than the Meltons. **Why is this?**

The Robinsons spend time managing their money but not worrying about it. Although they never inherited a dime, Mr. and Mrs. Robinson feel they can easily send their children to college. The $250,000 they have saved is also a good start for their retirement. Both are

working to improve their future income. Mr. Robinson is completing a college degree at night, and Mrs. Robinson has been taking weekend seminars offered at no cost by her employer. Both are hoping for promotions.

The Meltons are very worried about money. Their credit card balance keeps increasing every month. They have neither the time nor money to improve their education. Although they could sell their house for more than they owe on the mortgage, they have no savings. They hope their children will get scholarships to pay for college.

The Handy Dandy Guide

To solve the mystery of the two families, let's learn some basic points of economic reasoning that will help you make better choices. We summarize this approach to economic reasoning through the *Handy Dandy Guide*. It is based on six main ideas.

1. People choose.

This may seem obvious, but think for a minute about how many people say they "have no choice." In fact, we ALWAYS have a choice.

The Robinsons spend a few hours every week managing their money. They have a budget, record their expenses, and adjust their spending if they are "over budget." Their goal is to save 10 percent of their income each month. They investigate how to invest their savings, comparing rates of return and risks.

The Meltons feel they don't have time for this. They are thankful for their two credit cards because without them they could never get the things they want. The Meltons do spend a lot of time watching television; relaxing is important.

2. All choices involve costs.

Choices come with costs. Because the Robinsons spend time managing their money, they must give something up. Economists say there is an opportunity cost for every choice. The opportunity cost is the most valued option that you gave up because you chose what you did. The opportunity cost is your next best option.

For the Robinsons, the opportunity cost of managing their money is the television they give up. For the Meltons, the opportunity cost of watching television is managing their money.

Making good choices involves comparing the benefits and costs of any decision. The Robinsons are wealthier than the Meltons because of the choices they made.

3. People respond to incentives in predictable ways.

An incentive is a benefit or cost that influences a person's decisions.

One powerful incentive is money. Money is important because of the stuff we can buy with it and the freedom it gives us to make more choices. People work to earn money, but they also work to accomplish their goals and have a satisfying career. By managing your money more carefully, you can keep more of the benefits of your hard work by having the money to accomplish other goals.

Another incentive is interest on savings. Most people would rather have something today than tomorrow. This is why people pay interest when they borrow money and earn interest when they save it.

The incentive for the Robinsons to save is that they will have more goods and services in the future. They will also be able to achieve other goals because they can help others, spend money on recreation, and have a greater variety of choices. This is also an incentive for getting a good education. With a good education, you will earn much more in the future, understand more about the world, and have more control over your life.

4. People create economic systems that influence choices and incentives.

The American economic system relies on markets, choices, and incentives. Americans are free to start a business, get an education, choose an occupation, and buy or not buy an incredible variety of goods and services. Americans may save or not save, rent an apartment or buy a house, buy a new car, a used car or no car, and use credit cards or pay cash. Every decision has costs and benefits. The system creates incentives that guide our behavior.

The American private-enterprise system has made the United States a land of choices and opportunities. These opportunities involve ever-present tradeoffs and choices. Of course, every choice has an opportunity cost.

The Robinsons take better advantage of the opportunities available to them. They do not view themselves as victims of too little income or of businesses that charge too high prices. Instead, they make choices to increase their future income and spend that income wisely.

5. People gain when they trade voluntarily.

"Voluntary" refers to doing something because you want to, not because someone forced you. Neither the Robinsons nor the Meltons are forced to buy goods and services. They are not forced to work for their employers. They do these things because the benefits are greater than the costs.

Of course, things can go wrong when people trade. If you don't trade carefully and gather sound information, you may find you don't benefit as much from the trade as you expected. The Robinsons take more time than the Meltons before making such decisions.

6. People's choices have consequences that lie in the future.

If you watch television and read newspaper and magazine advertisements, you may think everyone lives for today. Most people, however, also live for tomorrow. Otherwise, why would we conserve, save, and invest?

Life is not a lottery. Sound decision making—not luck—will affect your future. The choices you make today will affect your future.

The Robinsons have more wealth because they saved more and spent less than the Meltons, even though the Meltons work more. The Robinsons also get more for their income because they compare costs, benefits, and alternatives before making major purchases. Their past decisions have affected their present wealth and lifestyle.

Questions

1. What is an opportunity cost?

2. Why is opportunity cost important when you make choices?

3. Why do people want to be wealthy?

4. What difference does it make if the United States is viewed as a land of victims or a land of opportunities?

5. What is the incentive for saving?

6. Why are the Robinsons wealthier than the Meltons?

The Boring School Mystery

Most high school students believe school is boring. Yet most students graduate from high school. Why do students stay in school if school is so boring? Can the Handy Dandy Guide **provide the answer to this mystery?**

There are many reasons to stay in school and many reasons to drop out. Yet many more students stay in school than drop out. For each of the following clues, put "S" for "stay in school" or "D" for "drop out of school." Then use the *Handy Dandy Guide* to explain why more people stay in school than drop out.

1. _____ High school dropouts can help their families earn more money for food, shelter, and transportation than their friends in high school.

2. _____ High school graduates have higher future incomes than high school dropouts.

3. _____ High school graduates can go to college.

4. _____ High school students must follow school rules, which limit freedom.

5. _____ High school dropouts can work full-time and have a better car, clothes, and social life than their friends in high school.

6. _____ Parents want their children to stay in school.

7. _____ School activities, such as sports and music, are fun for many students.

8. _____ Increased knowledge opens up increased choices.

Questions

1. What is the cost of staying in school?

2. What is the cost of dropping out of school?

Questions (continued)

3. What is the incentive for staying in school?

4. How does the American economic system encourage people to graduate from high school?

5. Is going to high school voluntary or do you have no choice?

6. Why do some students choose to drop out of school?

7. Why do most students choose to stay in high school and graduate?

8. What are the future consequences of a decision to drop out of school or stay in school?

Financial Fitness for Life: Bringing Home the Gold Student Workouts, ©National Council on Economic Education

Decision Making

A fundamental law of economics states that there is no such thing as a free lunch. There is no such thing as a free lunch because individuals, businesses, governments, and economic systems all face scarcity. Therefore, we must make decisions at the personal, business, and government levels. A wise decision involves weighing the benefits and costs of the alternatives. There is a cost to every decision.

Scarcity occurs because our resources are limited and our wants are unlimited. Scarcity exists because human wants always outstrip the limited resources available to satisfy them.

People's **wants** are never satisfied. No matter what we already have, we would like to have more. The United States is one of the richest nations in the world, but poverty still exists. Even wealthy individuals desire more. Few of us are satisfied with our education, health care, and standard of living. Many people would also like to have more income. Our wants are limited only by our imagination. Wants also change over time. Twenty years ago, few Americans had CD players, DVD players, cell phones, or computers. No one wanted a faster Internet connection.

Unfortunately, our **resources** are limited. We have only so many human resources, natural resources, and capital resources. **Human resources** are the physical, intellectual, and creative talents of people. When you get a better education, you improve your human resources. When a nation is better educated, it has more human resources—and a higher standard of living.

Natural resources are gifts of nature. Natural resources include water, forests, natural gas, oil, and climate. Natural resources are not the only resources a nation needs to become rich.

Capital resources include all the resources made and used by people to produce and distribute goods and services. Tools, factories, and office buildings are examples of capital resources. In economics, capital refers to items used to produce something else, not money. Money is just a medium of exchange used to make the buying and selling of goods and services easier. People like more money because they can use it to buy more stuff. It's the stuff that is important.

Because of scarcity, we must make choices. Every choice involves an **opportunity cost**. The opportunity cost of a decision is the next best alternative that is not chosen. It is the value of what you give up in order to get what you want.

11

Questions

1. Why is there no such thing as a free lunch?

2. Give some examples of natural resources, human resources, and capital resources.

    A. Natural resources

    B. Human resources

    C. Capital resources

3. What is capital?

4. Why do economists NOT view capital as money?

5. What is an opportunity cost?

Financial Fitness for Life: Bringing Home the Gold Student Workouts, ©National Council on Economic Education

Personal Decision Making

This exercise focuses on personal decision making. Our <u>personal resources</u> include time, money, and skills that we use to satisfy our wants. We use our personal resources to purchase goods and services. <u>Goods</u> are things we can touch, such as cars, houses, computers, and cell phones. <u>Services</u> are activities such as rock concerts, education, movies, insurance, loans, vacations, and health care. Of course, we cannot have all the goods and services we want because of scarcity. But we can have more goods and services if we choose wisely. By carefully considering the costs and benefits of our decisions, we can improve our lives.

A College for Maria

Maria Delgado will graduate from high school this spring. She plans to attend college, but she does not know which college to attend. She is using a decision-making model in order to make a better choice. Let's work through Maria's decision using the five-step decision-making model.

STEP 1: *Define the Problem*

Maria must recognize the problem. She knows all colleges and universities are not alike, and she must choose the one that is right for her. She plans to major in marketing.

STEP 2: *List the Alternatives*

Maria has found three main alternatives. State U is a big university with 30,000 students, and it offers both undergraduate and graduate programs. Many undergraduate classes are very large; some have more than 300 students. The tuition is reasonable. The business school and the marketing program are highly ranked nationally. State U is located 150 miles from Maria's hometown.

Local Community College is a two-year college only a few miles away from Maria's house. Its classes are smaller than State U's, averaging about 40 students. There are marketing classes. While some faculty members are outstanding, Maria has heard that most do not have Ph.D.s like they do at State U. The tuition for LCC is low, and if she decides on LCC, Maria could keep her part-time job.

13

Private College, which has only 3,000 students, is located 200 miles from Maria's hometown in a neighboring state. The classes are small, and the students get a lot of individual attention and help. The college offers marketing courses. Its admission standards are high, but Maria is an outstanding student and thinks she has a good chance of being accepted. Tuition is expensive. Private College gives scholarships and loans, but the cost would still be higher than at State U.

STEP 3: *Identify Your Criteria*

Your criteria are personal goals you feel are important. Every person has different criteria. Maria's most important criteria are these:

- Low-cost tuition because her family is not wealthy.
- High quality education, particularly in marketing.
- Small class size and personal attention.
- Close location to home because she feels she would miss her friends.

STEP 4: *Evaluate Your Alternatives*

Maria must now evaluate her alternatives against her criteria. She has decided to use the decision-making grid shown on page 14. She will use a "+" and "-" system to evaluate each alternative. One plus sign is positive and two plus signs are even better—very positive. A minus sign is negative. Complete the grid before going to Step 5.

STEP 5: *Make a Decision*

Maria decided to attend Local Community College for two years. Cost is very important to her. By attending the community college while working part-time, she might even be able to save some money. She felt the private college had the best program for her, but it is too expensive and too far from home. The community college had the most pluses. Low cost and closeness to home were very important to her, and the community college did best on these criteria.

Maria's Decision-Making Grid

Based on the information in this exercise, use the grid to help Maria make a decision. Then answer the questions that follow.

What is the problem?_____

Fill in the boxes with + , ++ , or −, as you think Maria might have decided.

ALTERNATIVES	CRITERIA			
	Low Cost	Quality Program	Personal Attention	Close to Home
State U				
Local Community College				
Private College				

What choice do you recommend for Maria based on her criteria?

Questions

1. Why is the decision-making model important?

2. Are there any additional criteria that Maria did not consider that you feel are important in choosing a college?

3. Do you agree with Maria? Why or why not?

Buying a New PC

You can use the decision-making model and grid for any consumer decision. Assume you want to buy a personal computer. Fill out the decision-making grid that follows and decide which PC to buy. Find the alternative models at electronics superstores, computer stores, or online computer services. Develop your criteria, which could include memory, hard disk capacity, modem speed, audio and video capabilities, and processing speed. Choose the criteria that are most important to you; fill out the grid; make a choice; and justify it.

PC Decision-Making Grid

The Problem: _____

CRITERIA ▶ ▼ ALTERNATIVES				

The Decision: _____

THEME 2

Education Pays Off: Learn Something
OVERVIEW

How much have you thought about what occupation you will seek after leaving school? Not much? That is not unusual. Even if you are among the few who have a plan, you will probably reexamine it several times over the next months and years.

Finding a job is important. Many high school students have part-time jobs and may be familiar with the process of finding a job. However, finding a job after technical school or college is different from finding a part-time job while you are still in high school. The usual routine in finding a full-time job is to write a letter of application, prepare a resume, complete a job application, and cross your fingers, hoping that you will be offered a job interview.

What sort of occupation is right for you? There are abundant sources of information about various occupations and how to find job openings. The *Occupational Outlook Handbook* in your school library or at **www.bls.gov** is a great source of information about what occupations pay and how much education is required. Similarly, there are many sources of job openings from your local newspaper to web sites on the Internet.

Not everyone, however, works for someone else. Some people prefer working for themselves. Do you enjoy being independent? Do you have a high level of energy? Do you like to work hard and see projects through to completion? If so, then perhaps you ought to consider starting your own business. After all, there are many opportunities out there for you to be your own boss.

Financial Fitness for Life: Bringing Home the Gold Student Workouts, ©National Council on Economic Education

Ever notice how people in some occupations earn more money than others? Michael Dell is worth billions while people who run gourmet coffee shops earn a whole lot less. Why is that? One of the main explanations has to do with an individual's level of education. Economists call education and training "human capital." On average, people who have higher levels of education earn more, sometimes significantly more, than those with lower levels of formal education. For example, people who graduate from high school earn more than those who do not. People who have some college usually earn more income than people who never go to college. Decisions about education should be looked upon as an investment in your human capital. Investing time and effort in your education will provide you good returns in the form of higher income over many years.

If you work a part-time job, perhaps you had a rude surprise when you received your first paycheck. You might have figured that your paycheck would simply be the total of the number of hours worked multiplied by your hourly rate of pay. Many young people are surprised to learn about deductions from their paychecks. Some of these deductions are optional, but many are mandatory. Optional deductions might be contributions to a company retirement plan. Mandatory deductions are payments for income taxes and Social Security. Uncle Sam takes a bite!

Questions

1. What are some steps involved in getting a job?

2. If you want to earn a living, do you have to work for someone else?

3. Is there a payoff for investing in your education?

Financial Fitness for Life: Bringing Home the Gold Student Workouts, ©National Council on Economic Education

Questions (continued)

4. Is your paycheck the total number of hours worked times your rate of pay?

FAQs

ABOUT EDUCATION PAYS OFF: LEARN SOMETHING

1. What are sources of job information?

The Occupational Outlook Handbook *produced by the Bureau of Labor Statistics, available online at **www.bls.gov** or in book form in the reference section of the library, provides lots of information on many occupations. Information includes the nature of the work, potential employers, working conditions, advancement potential, employment outlook, required education and training, and salary ranges.*

2. What are the advantages and disadvantages of owning your own business?

The advantages to becoming an entrepreneur include control of your own business success and the potential for significant income. The disadvantages are that business owners usually work long hours and at every job in the business, from manager to janitor. Pay is often low in the beginning, and vacations tend to be rare.

3. Where can you learn more about education beyond high school?

*Visit with your school guidance counselor. Guidance counselors usually have lots of information on educational opportunities in your community, state, and nation. Numerous web sites offer information on careers and college. Try **www.parkland.ccc.il.us/ccc/planning.html** to get started.*

4. What is the difference between gross pay and net pay?

Gross pay is the total amount of money earned. For an hourly employee, it is the hourly wage multiplied by the number of hours worked. Net pay is gross pay minus deductions. Deductions include federal, state, and local income taxes, Social Security contributions, and optional benefits like medical and life insurance, retirement savings, and profit sharing.

19

The Job Application Process

Employers in recent years have been experimenting with new ways to attract employees. But most employers still tend to follow similar procedures for recruiting and hiring new employees. People who are familiar with these procedures and are able to follow them have advantages in the job-seeking process over others who are less familiar with them.

STEP 1: *Looking for Job Openings*

There are several sources of job opportunities. One important source to consider is *America's Job Bank* (**www.ajb.dni.us**). It is the most extensive service available. *America's Job Bank* is offered by the U.S Department of Labor in partnership with state-operated employment services. *America's Job Bank* is a computerized network that links state employment services offices to provide job seekers with a pool of active job opportunities. Job seekers can search for job openings and submit resumes for employers to examine. Job seekers may research jobs within 25 miles of their homes, within counties, states, and throughout the United States. The job openings and resumes found in *America's Job Bank* are available on the Internet in many public libraries, colleges, universities, high schools, shopping malls, transition offices on military bases, and elsewhere.

Individuals increasingly are using *networking* as a less formal way of finding out about career opportunities. How might you uncover job opportunities using your personal network? Consider communicating by telephone or e-mail with friends and family members who, in turn, might be able to connect you to a potential employer. Make efforts to contact people who might know other people. Contact organizations that might help. For example, local employers often are members of a local Chamber of Commerce. These employers are often seeking new employees. Very likely, people at your local Chamber of Commerce will have information about how you can contact local employers through formal and informal ways. Other networking ideas include joining organizations and clubs, attending business luncheon meetings, and taking classes or seminars where you might come into contact with potential employers.

There are many other good sources of job information. Teachers and guidance counselors may know of local sources of employment. Many high schools offer cooperative or work-experience programs. Most post secondary education institutions, such as technical schools, colleges, and universities, have career placement offices. These offices often post job openings, may offer workshops on job-seeking skills, and may arrange for recruiters to interview students on campus.

Many communities have public and private employment agencies whose business is to help you find jobs for which you are prepared.

Don't forget to check out the classified "Help Wanted" notices in your local newspaper. Finally, businesses and government organizations often circulate job openings. They might be posted on bulletin boards or circulated among the offices.

STEP TWO: *The Letter of Application*

Job applicants often send a letter of application and a resume to a potential employer. The letter of application introduces you to the employer and allows you to tell the employer what you have to offer. A letter of application includes the normal characteristics of a business letter (typed, centered on page, and standard English). A typical letter expresses your interest in a particular job, links your experience, interest, or training to the job, and explains how you can be reached for an interview.

STEP THREE: *The Resume*

A resume is a summary of your work-related experiences. It presents your name, telephone number, street address, e-mail address, career objective, education, work experience, abilities, and other information, such as awards, extracurricular activities (club, sports, etc), offices held in organizations, and any special interests. A resume should tell the employer who you are in a neat, concise, and accurate way. If you wish, you can list references (names and addresses) on the resume. References are people who can tell a prospective employer about your work habits, character, and skills.

STEP FOUR: *The Application*

Employers ordinarily ask you to complete an employment application when you inquire about a job. When possible, you should type the application and return it to the employer. Many times, however, employers want you to complete the information on the spot. In this case, here are a few tips:

✔ Be sure to bring basic information such as your Social Security number, driver's license, and copies of necessary licenses or permits. Also, be sure to bring your resume and, if possible, a school transcript.

✔ Print clearly in the spaces provided. Use a good quality black or blue pen.

✔ Fill in all the blanks on the form. Write NA for not available or does not apply, when appropriate, so the employer knows that you did not skip parts of the form.

✔ Be truthful. Give complete answers.

STEP FIVE: *The Interview*

It is typical for an interested employer to contact you and arrange for a job interview. The job interview is a procedure in which you may be questioned about the statements you made in the application. The interview also allows the employer to gather other job-related information from you. Here are a few tips to consider as you prepare for a job interview.

✔ Find out about the company or agency. Often, companies have Internet sites or brochures that provide information on their mission and organization.

✔ Make a list of questions to ask about information that you want to obtain such as work schedules, benefits, and pay.

✔ Arrive on time or a little early. Never be late. Go alone.

Continued

✔ Be neat and clean. Dress modestly and conservatively.

✔ Do not overuse jewelry or fragrances.

✔ Do not smoke or chew gum.

✔ Be poised and confident. It is normal to be nervous, but try your best to appear relaxed.

✔ Do not appear overconfident or arrogant.

✔ Greet the interviewer with a firm handshake.

✔ Establish eye contact.

✔ Concentrate on clear communication. Speak clearly. Avoid slang or improper language. Listen carefully. Don't interrupt. Be responsive and truthful.

✔ Be ready for some open-ended questions. "Tell me about your qualifications for this job" or "Describe the ideal candidate for this position" are two possibilities.

✔ Emphasize your strong points. Be ready to be asked about your strengths as well as weaknesses.

✔ Be positive, upbeat, and enthusiastic.

Questions

1. **What are the five primary steps of getting a job?**

2. **What are two suggestions for finding a job?**

Questions (continued)

3. What are two tips for writing a letter of application?

4. What information is ordinarily included on a resume?

5. There are many suggestions for how best to conduct yourself at a job interview. Which suggestions do you think are most important?

Sample
Job Application

Below is a typical job application. Examine it to see how easy it would be for you to complete the application today. Answer the questions found after the form.

JOB APPLICATION

Today's date _____

PERSONAL INFORMATION *(please print clearly)*

Name: _____   Tel. # ( ) _____
          Last   First   Middle   Area Code

E-mail address: _____

Address: _____
                                   City   State   Zip

Date of birth _____   Social Security No. _____

Are you employed now?   ☐ Yes ☐ No   If yes, where?
_____

In case of emergency notify:

Name: _____   Tel. # ( ) _____
          Last   First   Middle   Area Code

Address:
_____
                                   City   State   Zip

AVAILABILITY

Are you legally able to be employed in the U.S. ?   ☐ Yes ☐ No

What type of position are you seeking?   ☐ Part-time ☐ Full-time

                      M   T   W   T   F   S   S

Hours   From: _____

Available   To: _____

How will you get to work? _____

Page 1 of 3 *continued on page 2*

EDUCATION

School name and location: _____

Total # years attended: _____ Did you graduate? _____ GPA _____

Degree, major or total hours: _____

High school: _____ ❑ Yes ❑ No

Trade or business school: _____ ❑ Yes ❑ No

College/university: _____ ❑ Yes ❑ No

EMPLOYMENT HISTORY

1. Company _____

Address: _____ Tel. # ( ) _____
                    City   State   Zip   Area Code

Position: _____ Supervisor: _____

Dates worked: From: _____ To: _____

Wage: _____ Reason for leaving: _____

2. Company _____

Address: _____ Tel. # ( ) _____
                    City   State   Zip   Area Code

Position: _____ Supervisor: _____

Dates worked: From: _____ To: _____

Wage: _____ Reason for leaving: _____

SKILLS *(Complete if applying for clerical, secretarial, or data processing position.)*

Keyboarding: ❑ Yes ___ WPM ❑ No   Word processing: ❑ Yes ___ WPM ❑ No

Spreadsheets ❑ Yes ❑ No   Data entry ❑ Yes ❑ No

Desk top publishing ❑ Yes ❑ No   Web site experience ❑ Yes ❑ No

Word processing software (specify)

_____

Spreadsheet software *(specify)*

_____

List other skills, professional certifications, or training which you feel qualify you for the position for which you are applying.

_____

continued on page 3

REFERENCES *(other than relatives)*

Name _____ Occupation _____ Tel. # ( )_____

Address:

_____
City   State   Zip

Name _____ Occupation _____ Tel. # ( )_____

Address:

_____
City   State   Zip

SIGNATURE

I declare the information provided by me in this application is true, correct, and complete to the best of my knowledge. I understand that if employed, any falsification, misstatement, or omission of fact in connection to my application, whether on this document or not, may result in immediate termination of employment.

I authorize the references listed above to give you any and all information concerning my previous or current employment and any pertinent information they may have, personal or otherwise, and release all parties from all liability from any damage that may result from furnishing the same to you.

I acknowledge that employment may be conditional upon successful completion of a substance abuse screening test as part of the company's pre-employment policy.

I understand it is unlawful to require or administer a lie detector test as a condition of employment or continued employment. An employer who violates this law shall be subject to criminal and/or civil liabilities.

_____   _____
Applicant Signature   Date

AMERICANS WITH DISABILITIES

Most of the information provided by potential employees to potential employers is routine and job related. However, Title I of the Americans with Disabilities Act requires that individuals with disabilities make known to employers that they need special accommodations such as a Braille cash register or a desk that has wheelchair access, in order to do the tasks that are required for the job. To the best of their ability, employers are to make these accommodations for applicants who meet all other job requirements.

INFORMATION RIGHTS

The vast majority of employers only want to establish how your background matches their job requirements. However, some employers may stray into asking about non-job-related information. Some areas of information are off-limits for the job application and the job interview. With rare exceptions, federal law prohibits hiring decisions being made on the basis of race, color, national origin, religion, gender, pregnancy, marital status, parenthood, age, height, weight, criminal record, or perceived disability. Interviewers and job applications are not allowed to pose personal questions that do not pertain to the requirements of the job.

Questions

1. What information is requested on the job application?

2. What are the obligations of individuals with disabilities?

3. What sort of questions are employers not supposed to ask?

Job Postings and Interview Form

WE ARE SEEKING DEPENDABLE INDIVIDUALS WHO CAN GROW WITH OUR COMPANY. WE OFFER FULL-TIME AND PART-TIME POSITIONS WITH A VARIETY OF SHIFTS AND SCHEDULES. PREVIOUS EXPERIENCE WITH THESE JOBS WILL BE HELPFUL.

ADMINISTRATIVE ASSISTANT

Supports managers by answering phones, typing correspondence, and coordinating travel schedules and meetings. Must be able to handle a variety of tasks under deadline. Skills required include word processing and an attention to detail.

CASHIER

Conducts customer transactions with speed, accuracy, and efficiency while meeting or exceeding service quality standards. Accepts express transactions from clients, such as deposits, withdrawals, transfers, and checks to be cashed. Sets up, closes, and balances cash at station. Bilingual skills a plus.

DATA ENTRY OPERATOR

Posts transactions to online computer system. Creates specific reports as requested. Skills required include 10-key adding machine, accurate data entry, typing.

LINE AND PREP COOK

Responsible for preparing quality food in fast-paced kitchen. Skills: Ability to follow exacting preparation standards; teamwork with other kitchen and wait staff to provide high-quality food and service to customers.

MACHINE OPERATOR

Operates statement-rendering machine. Does minor repair work on machine. Skills: Must have good mechanical aptitude and be able to lift 10-20 pounds.

RESEARCH CLERK

Carries out interdepartmental research. Reconciles a general ledger accounting system to a variety of sources. Determines charges to customers for research inquiries.

Verifies errors and makes adjustments. Good verbal and written skills are a must, along with the ability to learn quickly and follow directions. Skills required include accounting, calculator, and personal computer.

WAREHOUSE DRIVER

Responsible for delivering orders. Must have attractive personality for customer interaction, good driving record, and knowledge of city and suburbs.

WE OFFER COMPETITIVE SALARIES AND COMPREHENSIVE BENEFITS PACKAGE, INCLUDING MEDICAL/DENTAL, LIFE INSURANCE, RETIREMENT PLAN, CHILD CARE ASSISTANCE, AND PAID VACATIONS AND HOLIDAYS.

WE ARE AN EQUAL OPPORTUNITY EMPLOYER.

Interviewer Evaluation Form

Name of applicant: _____

Interviewed by: _____

Position applied for: _____

SAMPLE INTERVIEW QUESTIONS

- Why are you applying for this job?
- What about the job most appeals to you?
- What about the job, if anything, does not appeal to you?
- What are your qualifications for this position?
- What experiences do you have that will be helpful to you in this job?
- What are your strengths?
- What are your weaknesses?
- What would you like to be doing five years from now, and how do you think this job can help you get there?
- Is there anything else I should know about you in considering you for this position?

INTERVIEWER'S EVALUATION

The job applicant: (check all that apply)

- ☐ Seemed prepared for the interview
- ☐ Appeared confident
- ☐ Communicated clearly
- ☐ Was able to relate strengths and/or experiences to job needs

The job application: (check all that apply)

- ☐ Was neatly prepared and presented
- ☐ Was thorough
- ☐ Did a good job of highlighting the candidate's strengths and skills

The things that most impress me about this job applicant are:

The areas in which this candidate might improve are:

Sample Letter of Application

234 Elm Tree Road
Berlin, WI 54232-4232
(920) 123-4444

June 15, 2001

Ms. R. B. Posnanski, Manager
Wildlife Unlimited
2400 Hartford Avenue
Milwaukee, WI 53123 - 0123

Dear Ms. Posnanski:

Please consider me an applicant for the clerical assistant position advertised in last Sunday's *Journal Sentinel.*

My high school course work in business, which included word processing, accounting, and computer studies, has prepared me for an entry-level position. Enclosed is my resume that lists my education, experience, and skills.

My long-range goal is to work in an office where I can accept increasing responsibilities and advance toward a position as an administrative assistant. I gained valuable knowledge and experience in my high school and while working at Wal-Mart in Berlin, Wisconsin.

Please call me to set up a time for an interview. I can be reached at (920) 123-4444.

I look forward to hearing from you.

Sincerely,

Kelly A. Thomas

Kelly A. Thomas
Enclosure: resume

30

ILLUSTRATION 4.2

ILLUSTRATION 4.2

Sample Resume

KELLY A. THOMAS
234 Elm Tree Road
Berlin, WI 54232-4232
(920) 123-4444

CAREER OBJECTIVE
Office or accounting clerk position with the opportunity for advancement to administrative assistant.

EDUCATION
1997-2001 Berlin High School, Berlin, Wisconsin (GPA 3.33)

Major Course of Study: Business and Accounting

Relevant Course Work
Word Processing
Database Applications
Business Law

Accounting I and II
Business Communications
Personal Finance

Relevant Skills
Typing (70 wpm)
Word processing and
Spreadsheet applications

Extracurricular Activities
Member: Future Business Leaders of America, 2000
Competitor at regional skills event in area of accounting

Recognition
Received highest attendance award in high school (missed 1.5 days out of 4 years)

WORK HISTORY
Cashier, Wal-Mart, Berlin, Wisconsin (six months, part-time)
• Greet customers, operate cash register, and balance cash register.

Material Handler, Jesse Jackets, Oshkosh, Wisconsin (summer help)
• Check garments for mistakes or flaws and fix them, take garments to appropriate departments.

Office Assistant, Berlin High School, Berlin, Wisconsin (one year, part-time)
• Work in the front office included helping new students get to classes, answering the telephone, running errands, typing forms, and calling parents.

REFERENCES Provided on request.

31

Take the Test

Complete the questionnaire below. Read each statement on the left and place an X in the column that reflects whether you agree or disagree with the statement and how strongly you agree or disagree. There are no right or wrong answers.

Statement	1 Strongly Disagree	2 Disagree	3 Agree	4 Strongly Agree
1. I sometimes enjoy taking risks.				
2. I like to work hard at projects that interest me.				
3. I have a high level of energy.				
4. I want to achieve results based largely on my own efforts.				
5. I like being creative.				
6. I like to start projects on my own.				
7. I tend to see tasks through to completion.				
8. I am confident in my abilities.				
9. I am good at a lot of different tasks.				
10. I am interested in making lots of money.				
TOTALS				

Total Points = _____

When you have completed the questionnaire, notice that each response has a numeric rating. Add the total number of points of the ratings you have given each statement and write the total in the space below the questionnaire.

Who Are Entrepreneurs?

Most people work for others. Working for others, however, is not for everyone. Some individuals welcome the challenge of starting their own business and working for themselves. Research on entrepreneurs suggests that they share certain characteristics. Entrepreneurs tend to be willing to take risks. They are people who seem to enjoy being independent, leading, and being recognized. Among other things, entrepreneurs tend to be confident, hard working, well organized, and self-starters.

Conditions of Employment	Work for Someone Else in Corporation	Work for Yourself
Job Stability	Job stability depends largely on the success of the division, department, or immediate superiors.	Job stability depends nearly completely on the success of the business.
Work Hours	Often long but somewhat predictable.	Very long but self-determined.
Personal Success	Your success depends largely on the success of the company, department, or superiors.	Your personal success depends nearly completely on the success of the business.
Salary	Usually set in a pre-determined range for the department of position reflecting market conditions for the job. Raises are given after predictable periods of time.	Low in the beginning. Entrepreneurs often take little in the beginning so that most income can be put back into the business. The level depends on the success of the business.
Benefits	A standard package of benefits or menu of benefits within the standard package is often provided. Jobs often include major medical insurance and perhaps other coverage. Paid vacations, personal and sick days are often included. Some type of retirement program such as a 401k program is available.	Benefits are provided by the business. Benefits are often not as generous as might be available in a corporation. Vacations tend to be rare and tend to mean lost income.
Job Responsibilities	Responsibilities are usually explained in the employee handbook but may change as conditions in the company change.	Entrepreneurs must be prepared to do everything. Bookkeeping, selling, cleaning, painting, and producing items are likely to be included.

EXERCISE 5.2 Continued

Questions

1. What are some of the characteristics of entrepreneurs?

2. Is corporate life for you or is running a small business more appealing? Identify three ways in which working in a corporation differs from working for yourself.

Hear a Business Opportunity Knocking on Your Door?

Small businesses operate in every sector of the economy. There are many opportunities for entrepreneurs, especially in the service area. Examine the chart below. Complete it with your thoughts about what sort of business opportunities might exist for new entrepreneurs in services to individual households, retail services, franchise businesses, and providing services via the Internet.

Services to Individual Households	Retail Services	Franchise	Internet Sales and Services
In-home child care	Shoe store	Gas station	Creating web sites
Lawn and tree care	Drug store	Fast food	Book sales

I Wonder Why Nobody Ever Made a...?

1. Describe a good or service you think consumers want. It might be an existing good or service provided in a new way. Or your idea might be an original idea for a good or service.

2. What consumers do you think might be interested in this good or service? Name your customers.

3. How would you produce the good or service you have in mind?

4. How many people would you need to hire to get started? What might their jobs be?

5. Where might you find money to start up your new business? Personal savings? Loans from friends or family? Bank loans?

6. Develop a one-minute commercial for your good or service. You might wish to design a sign, write a jingle, or create a slogan that would catch the attention of customers and encourage them to buy your good or service.

36

EXERCISE
6.1

Why Some Jobs Pay More Than Others

Read the following material, and study Table 1. Then answer the questions at the end of the exercise.

Not everyone makes the same amount of income. *Forbes Magazine* reported in 1999 that among the top 50 wealthiest people in the nation are such individuals as Michael Dell and Robert (Ted) Turner. They were worth billions of dollars. The *Forbes Magazine* Celebrity 100 for 2000 set the earnings of Oprah Winfrey at $150 million, Shaquille O'Neal at $31 million, and Venus Williams at $5 million. The Bureau of Labor Statistics reports that the 1998 median net annual earnings of medical doctors was $164,000. The 1998 median annual earnings of registered nurses was $40,690. The 1998 average teacher earned $39,300. The 1998 median annual earnings of full-time cosmetologists was $15,150, excluding tips.

The money that a person receives in exchange for work or use of property is called income. Income can come from many sources. People hold a combination of resources that can be used to produce income. These resources may include savings, stocks, land, rental property. However, most of the income that people earn in the United States comes from labor. Wages and other labor income make up about 75 percent of every dollar of total income.

What causes earnings to vary so much from one occupation to another?

One factor is the market for different occupations. For example, demand for dental hygienists is expected to grow much faster than average for all occupations due in part to increasing demand for dental care. This change in demand will probably cause wages for dental hygienists to increase. In contrast, demand for announcers for radio and television stations is expected to decline. This change in demand will probably cause wages for announcers to decrease.

As you might expect, other factors also contribute to differences in earnings. People with more natural ability in their occupation tend to make more money than those with less natural ability. People who work hard earn more income than people who don't work hard. People who get along with others and are self-disciplined tend to earn more income than people who are hard to get along with or are less disciplined.

An important factor related to income is investing in human capital. Human capital is investing in people primarily through education and training. The most important type of human capital is education. Workers with more human capital—in this case more education—tend to earn more income than people with less education. Gary Becker, recipient of the 1992 Nobel Memorial Prize in Economic Science, has explained that gaining a high school and college education raises a person's income even after taking out the direct costs (e.g., tuition and books) and the indirect costs (e.g., income that could have made while in school) of getting an education. High school and college education raises a person's income regardless of intelligence or family wealth.

The U.S. Census Bureau reports on the relationship between level of formal education and income. **Please examine Table 1 on the next page and respond to the questions that follow.**

EXERCISE 6.1

Continued

Table 1 LEVEL OF FORMAL EDUCATION AND INCOME	
Level of Education	**Average Median Income Males and Females Aged 25 and Older, 1998**
Less than 9th grade	$16,343
9th to 12th grade, no diploma	19,643
High school graduate (includes GED)	26,325
Some college, no degree	30,986
Associate's degree	33,430
Bachelor's degree	42,695
Master's degree	51,085
Professional degree	73,065
Doctorate degree	60,678

Source: *Money Income in the United States: Current Population Reports*
U.S. Census Bureau, issued September, 2000

Questions

1. What is income?

2. What factors other than education contribute to an increased income from work?

3. What is human capital?

Questions (continued)

4. Examine Table 1. Describe the relationship between education and income from work. Does education pay?

5. In 1998, how much more would a high school graduate expect to earn per year than an 11th-grade dropout?

6. Assuming a 40-year work life and no pay increases, how much more might a high school graduate expect to earn over a lifetime than an 11th-grade dropout?

7. Does it pay to stay in school one more year and graduate? Why?

8. In 1998, how much more would a college graduate expect to earn per year than a high school graduate?

9. Assuming a 40-year work life and no pay increases, how much more might a college graduate expect to earn than a high school graduate over a lifetime?

10. Is education a good investment?

Financial Fitness for Life: Bringing Home the Gold Student Workouts, ©National Council on Economic Education

EXERCISE 6.2

Education and Training

Answer the questions at the end of the exercise after you have read and analyzed the material.

What jobs are growing the fastest? It is hard to predict. The U.S. Bureau of Labor Statistics (BLS), however, studies how job markets are changing. The BLS reports that many of the fastest-growing jobs will require education and training beyond a high school diploma. The BLS reports that employment in occupations that do not require post secondary education are projected to grow by about 12 percent from 1998 to 2008. Occupations that require at least a bachelor's degree are projected to grow at almost 22 percent.

Education is essential in getting and keeping a high-paying job. However, the BLS reports further that a number of occupations (such as blue-collar work supervisors, electricians, and police patrol officers) do not require a college degree, yet offer higher than average earnings.

Level of Education Required for Fastest-Growing Occupations

Source: *Bureau of Labor Statistics, 2000*

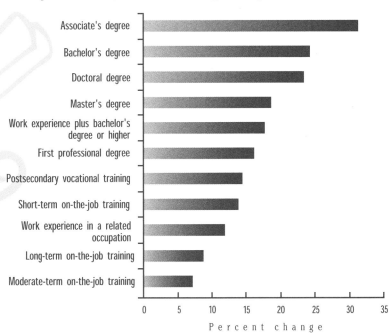

Questions

1. What three levels of formal education and training are associated with the fastest-growing jobs?

2. What three levels of training are associated with slower-growing jobs?

40

What Are All These Deductions from My Paycheck?

It's exciting to receive your first paycheck. But for many young people, that first rush of excitement soon yields to disappointment. They quickly realize the money they earned is not the same as the money they received. Uncle Sam and a lot of others have taken a bite out of that paycheck.

GROSS PAY

Gross pay is the total amount of money earned before any deductions are made. For example, many employees are paid at an hourly rate. In the case of an hourly employee, the record of hours worked is multiplied by the employee's hourly rate of pay. This results in the employee's gross pay.

40 hours x $7.00 an hour = $280.00
Gross pay = $280.00

Similar calculations are made to determine the gross pay of employees who receive a monthly or annual salary.

NET PAY

The amount left after all deductions are taken out of the gross pay is the *net pay*. This is the actual amount of an employee's paycheck. Net pay is often called take-home pay because it is the amount of money an employee actually receives on payday.

Gross pay
– Deductions
= Net pay

41

REQUIRED DEDUCTIONS

Federal income tax, state income tax, local taxes, and FICA are among the required deductions taken from an employee's paycheck. FICA is the abbreviation for Federal Insurance Contributions Act. FICA provides for a federal system of old-age, survivors, disability, and health-care insurance. The old-age, survivors, and disability portion is paid by the Social Security tax. The health-care insurance portion is paid by the Medicare tax.

The actual amount deducted from a paycheck for federal, state, and income taxes is determined by reference to tax tables provided by the various levels of government. Employers use the information provided by the tax tables and combine it with information from employees to determine how much to take out of an employee's paycheck. Employees complete the W-4 Form—Employee's Withholding Allowance Certificate—when they are hired. This form tells the employer the number of allowances the employee wishes to claim. For example, an employee is able to claim allowances for himself or herself, a spouse, and children under 21 years of age whom the employee supports. The more allowances an employee claims, the less money withheld from the employee's paycheck.

MANDATORY DEDUCTIONS FROM YOUR PAYCHECK		
Deduction	**What do you get?**	**Who pays?**
Federal income tax	Funds services provided by the federal government, such as defense, human services, and the monitoring and regulation of trade.	Employee
State income tax	Funds services provided by state government, such as roads, safety, and health. (Not all states levy an income tax.)	Employee
Local income tax	Funds services provided by the city or other local government, such as schools, police, and fire protection. (Not all areas levy an income tax.)	Employee
FICA: Social Security tax	Provides for old-age, survivors, and disability insurance.	Employee and employer
FICA: Medicare tax	Provides for certain health care insurance.	Employee and employer

Financial Fitness for Life: Bringing Home the Gold Student Workouts, ©National Council on Economic Education

OTHER DEDUCTIONS

In addition to required deductions, employers may take money directly out of employee paychecks to pay for various employee benefits. Benefits vary by industry, by business, and by the status of the employee in the firm. Benefits may include such things as life insurance, disability insurance, medical insurance, dental insurance, retirement savings plan, and profit-sharing.

OTHER DEDUCTIONS *		
Deduction	**What do you get?**	**Who pays?**
Life insurance	Pays a beneficiary in the event that an employee dies.	Employer or employee, or shared
Long-term disability insurance	Provides benefits in the event that an employee is completely disabled.	Employer or employee, or shared
Medical insurance	Employee and family insurance coverage for medical care expenses, including hospitalization, physician services, surgery, and major medical expenses.	Employer or employee, or shared
Dental insurance	Employee and family insurance coverage for dental care expenses, including preventive, diagnostic, basic, major, and orthodontic services.	Employer or employee, or shared
Retirement savings plan	A tax-deferred savings plan for retirement.	Employer or employee (Employer may match percentage.)
Charity	A donation to a specific charity	Employee (Employer may match a percentage of employee contribution.)

Whether or not these benefits are offered, and who will fund them, varies by the employer.

Financial Fitness for Life: Bringing Home the Gold Student Workouts, ©National Council on Economic Education

Continued

Questions

1. What is gross pay?

2. What is net pay?

3. Is your paycheck the total of the number of hours worked times the rate of pay?

4. Name three mandatory deductions.

5. Name three other deductions.

Calculating a Paycheck #1

Imagine that you are a new employee at Foo Foo Gourmet Coffee Shop.

Foo Foo pays its employees each week. You have claimed one allowance on your W-4 form. You are single. You work 40 hours per week at $7.00 per hour. Even as a beginning employee,

you can contribute up to $20 each week to a 401k retirement plan. Use the background information and the tax tables 7.1 and 7.2 and information on the form below to calculate your net pay.

Employee's name: _____

Pay period ☐ Weekly ☐ Bimonthly ☐ Monthly

Number of allowances _____ (0 or more) ☐ Single ☐ Married

GROSS PAY

1. Regular wages: _____ Hours at _____ per hour = _____

2. Regular salary _____ = _____

Gross Pay = _____

REQUIRED DEDUCTIONS

3. Federal Income Tax (see U.S. tax table) _____

4. State Income Tax (see state tax table) _____

5. FICA: Social Security Tax (use 6.20% x gross pay) _____

6. FICA: Medicare Tax (use 1.45% x gross pay) _____

OTHER DEDUCTIONS

7. Medical insurance _____

8. Disability insurance _____

9. Retirement (401k) _____

10. Credit union _____

11. Union dues _____

Total Deductions (total lines 3 through 11) _____

Net Pay (subtract total deductions from the gross pay) _____

45

Calculating a Paycheck #2

Imagine that you are a new assistant manager at Foo Foo Gourmet Coffee Shop.

Foo Foo pays its employees each week. You have claimed zero allowances on your W-4 form. You are single. You work 40 hours per week at $9.00 per hour. As an assistant manager, you can contribute up to $30 each week to a 401k retirement plan and pay $15 a week for health insurance. Use this background information, information on the form below, and the tax tables in Table 7.1 and 7.2 to calculate your net pay.

Employee's name: _____

Pay period ☐ Weekly ☐ Bimonthly ☐ Monthly

Number of allowances _____ (0 or more) ☐ Single ☐ Married

GROSS PAY

1. Regular wages: _____ Hours at _____ per hour = _____

2. Regular salary _____ = _____

                                            Gross Pay = _____

REQUIRED DEDUCTIONS

3. Federal Income Tax (see U.S. tax table) _____

4. State Income Tax (see state tax table) _____

5. FICA: Social Security Tax (use 6.20% x gross pay) _____

6. FICA: Medicare Tax (use 1.45% x gross pay) _____

OTHER DEDUCTIONS

7. Medical insurance _____

8. Disability insurance _____

9. Retirement (401k) _____

10. Credit union _____

11. Union dues _____

Total Deductions (total lines 3 through 11) _____

Net Pay (subtract total deductions from the gross pay) _____

Financial Fitness for Life: Bringing Home the Gold Student Workouts, ©National Council on Economic Education

TABLE 7.1

Federal Tax Table
Single Persons/Weekly Payroll Period

And the wages are —		And the number of withholding allowances claimed is —										
At least	But less than	0	1	2	3	4	5	6	7	8	9	10
		The amount of income tax to be withheld is —										
$0	$55	0	0	0	0	0	0	0	0	0	0	0
55	60	1	0	0	0	0	0	0	0	0	0	0
60	65	2	0	0	0	0	0	0	0	0	0	0
65	70	2	0	0	0	0	0	0	0	0	0	0
70	75	3	0	0	0	0	0	0	0	0	0	0
75	80	4	0	0	0	0	0	0	0	0	0	0
80	85	5	0	0	0	0	0	0	0	0	0	0
85	90	5	0	0	0	0	0	0	0	0	0	0
90	95	6	0	0	0	0	0	0	0	0	0	0
95	100	7	0	0	0	0	0	0	0	0	0	0
100	105	8	0	0	0	0	0	0	0	0	0	0
105	110	8	0	0	0	0	0	0	0	0	0	0
110	115	9	1	0	0	0	0	0	0	0	0	0
115	120	10	2	0	0	0	0	0	0	0	0	0
120	125	11	2	0	0	0	0	0	0	0	0	0
125	130	11	3	0	0	0	0	0	0	0	0	0
130	135	12	4	0	0	0	0	0	0	0	0	0
135	140	13	5	0	0	0	0	0	0	0	0	0
140	145	14	5	0	0	0	0	0	0	0	0	0
145	150	14	6	0	0	0	0	0	0	0	0	0
150	155	15	7	0	0	0	0	0	0	0	0	0
155	160	16	8	0	0	0	0	0	0	0	0	0
160	165	17	8	0	0	0	0	0	0	0	0	0
165	170	17	9	1	0	0	0	0	0	0	0	0
170	175	18	10	2	0	0	0	0	0	0	0	0
175	180	19	11	2	0	0	0	0	0	0	0	0
180	185	20	11	3	0	0	0	0	0	0	0	0
185	190	20	12	4	0	0	0	0	0	0	0	0
190	195	21	13	5	0	0	0	0	0	0	0	0
195	200	22	14	5	0	0	0	0	0	0	0	0
200	210	23	15	6	0	0	0	0	0	0	0	0
210	220	25	16	8	0	0	0	0	0	0	0	0
220	230	26	18	9	1	0	0	0	0	0	0	0
230	240	28	19	11	3	0	0	0	0	0	0	0
240	250	29	21	12	4	0	0	0	0	0	0	0
250	260	31	22	14	6	0	0	0	0	0	0	0
260	270	32	24	15	7	0	0	0	0	0	0	0
270	280	34	25	17	9	0	0	0	0	0	0	0
280	290	35	27	18	10	2	0	0	0	0	0	0
290	300	37	28	20	12	3	0	0	0	0	0	0
300	310	38	30	21	13	5	0	0	0	0	0	0
310	320	40	31	23	15	6	0	0	0	0	0	0
320	330	41	33	24	16	8	0	0	0	0	0	0
330	340	43	34	26	18	9	1	0	0	0	0	0
340	350	44	36	27	19	11	2	0	0	0	0	0
350	360	46	37	29	21	12	4	0	0	0	0	0
360	370	47	39	30	22	14	5	0	0	0	0	0
370	380	49	40	32	24	15	7	0	0	0	0	0
380	390	50	42	33	25	17	8	0	0	0	0	0
390	400	52	43	35	27	18	10	1	0	0	0	0
400	410	53	45	36	28	20	11	3	0	0	0	0
410	420	55	46	38	30	21	13	4	0	0	0	0
420	430	56	48	39	31	23	14	6	0	0	0	0
430	440	58	49	41	33	24	16	7	0	0	0	0
440	450	59	51	42	34	26	17	9	1	0	0	0
450	460	61	52	44	36	27	19	10	2	0	0	0
460	470	62	54	45	37	29	20	12	4	0	0	0
470	480	64	55	47	39	30	22	13	5	0	0	0
480	490	65	57	48	40	32	23	15	7	0	0	0
490	500	67	58	50	42	33	25	16	8	0	0	0
500	510	68	60	51	43	35	26	18	10	1	0	0
510	520	70	61	53	45	36	28	19	11	3	0	0
520	530	71	63	54	46	38	29	21	13	4	0	0
530	540	73	64	56	48	39	31	22	14	6	0	0
540	550	74	66	57	49	41	32	24	16	7	0	0
550	560	76	67	59	51	42	34	25	17	9	0	0
560	570	79	69	60	52	44	35	27	19	10	2	0
570	580	82	70	62	54	45	37	28	20	12	3	0
580	590	84	72	63	55	47	38	30	22	13	5	0
590	600	87	73	65	57	48	40	31	23	15	6	0

TABLE 7.2

State Tax Table
(Example)*

And the wages are —		And the number of withholding allowances claimed is —										
At least	But less than	0	1	2	3	4	5	6	7	8	9	10
		The amount of Wisconsin income tax to be withheld shall be —										
$ 0	$ 75	$ 0	$ 0	$ 0	$ 0	$ 0	$ 0	$ 0	$ 0	$ 0	$ 0	$ 0
75	80	.10										
80	85	.30										
85	90	.50	.20									
90	95	.80	.40	.10								
95	100	1.00	.60	.30								
100	105	1.20	.90	.50	.20							
105	110	1.50	110	.70	.40							
110	115	1.70	1.30	1.00	.60	.30						
115	120	1.90	1.60	1.20	.90	.50	.10					
120	125	2.10	1.80	1.40	1.10	.70	.40					
125	130	2.40	2.00	1.70	1.30	1.00	.60	.30				
130	135	2.60	2.30	1.90	1.50	1.20	.80	.50	.10			
135	140	2.80	2.50	2.10	1.80	1.40	1.10	.70	.40			
140	145	3.10	2.70	2.40	2.00	1.70	1.30	.90	.60	.20		
145	150	3.30	2.90	2.60	2.20	1.90	1.50	1.20	.80	.50	.10	
150	155	3.50	3.20	2.80	2.50	2.10	1.80	1.40	1.00	.70	.30	
155	160	3.80	3.40	3.00	2.70	2.30	2.00	1.60	1.30	.90	.60	.20
160	165	4.00	3.60	3.30	2.90	2.60	2.20	1.90	1.50	1.20	.80	.40
165	170	4.20	3.90	3.50	3.20	2.80	2.40	2.10	1.70	1.40	1.00	.70
170	175	4.40	4.10	3.70	3.40	3.00	2.70	2.30	2.00	1.60	1.30	.90
175	180	4.70	4.30	4.00	3.60	3.30	2.90	2.60	2.20	1.80	1.50	1.00
180	185	4.90	4.60	4.20	3.80	3.50	3.10	2.80	2.40	2.10	1.70	1.40
185	190	5.10	4.80	4.40	4.10	3.70	3.40	3.00	2.70	2.30	2.00	1.60
190	195	5.40	5.00	4.70	4.30	4.00	3.60	3.20	2.90	2.50	2.20	1.80
195	200	5.60	5.20	4.90	4.50	4.20	3.80	3.50	3.10	2.80	2.40	2.10
200	205	5.80	5.50	5.10	4.80	4.40	4.10	3.70	3.30	3.00	2.60	2.30
205	210	6.10	5.70	5.40	5.00	4.70	4.30	4.00	3.60	3.20	2.90	2.50
210	215	6.30	6.00	5.60	5.30	4.90	4.60	4.20	3.90	3.50	3.10	2.80
215	220	6.60	6.20	5.90	5.50	5.20	4.80	4.50	4.10	3.80	3.40	3.10
220	225	6.80	6.50	6.10	5.80	5.40	5.10	4.70	4.40	4.00	3.70	3.30
225	230	7.10	6.80	6.40	6.00	5.70	5.30	5.00	4.60	4.30	3.90	3.60
230	235	7.50	7.00	6.70	6.30	5.90	5.60	5.20	4.90	4.50	4.20	3.80
235	240	7.80	7.30	6.90	6.60	6.20	5.90	5.50	5.10	4.80	4.40	4.10
240	245	8.10	7.70	7.20	6.80	6.50	6.10	5.80	4.50	5.00	4.70	4.30
245	250	8.50	8.00	7.50	7.10	6.70	6.40	6.00	5.70	5.30	5.00	4.60
250	255	8.80	8.40	7.90	7.40	7.00	6.60	6.30	5.90	5.60	5.20	4.90
255	260	9.20	8.70	8.20	7.80	7.30	6.90	6.50	6.20	5.80	5.50	5.10
260	265	9.50	9.00	8.60	8.10	7.60	7.20	6.80	6.40	6.10	5.70	5.40
265	270	9.90	9.40	8.90	8.40	8.00	7.50	7.00	6.70	6.30	6.00	5.60
270	275	10.20	9.70	9.30	8.80	8.30	7.80	7.40	6.90	6.60	6.20	5.90
275	280	10.60	10.10	9.60	9.10	8.70	8.20	7.70	7.20	6.90	6.50	6.10
280	285	10.90	10.40	9.90	9.50	9.00	8.50	8.10	7.60	7.10	6.80	6.40
285	290	11.20	10.80	10.30	9.80	9.30	8.90	8.40	7.90	7.50	7.00	6.70
290	295	11.60	11.10	10.60	10.20	9.70	9.20	8.70	8.30	7.80	7.30	6.90
295	300	11.90	11.50	11.00	10.50	10.00	9.60	9.10	8.60	8.10	7.70	7.20
300	305	12.30	11.80	11.30	10.90	10.40	9.90	9.40	9.00	8.50	8.00	7.50
305	310	12.60	12.10	11.70	11.20	10.70	10.30	9.80	9.30	8.80	8.40	7.90
310	315	13.00	12.50	12.00	11.50	11.10	10.60	10.10	9.60	9.20	8.70	8.20
315	320	13.30	12.80	12.40	11.90	11.40	10.90	10.50	10.00	9.50	9.00	8.60
320	325	13.70	13.20	12.70	12.20	11.80	11.30	10.80	10.30	9.90	9.40	8.90
325	330	14.00	13.50	13.00	12.60	12.10	11.60	11.20	10.70	10.20	9.70	9.30
330	335	14.30	13.90	13.40	12.90	12.40	12.00	11.50	11.00	10.60	10.10	9.60
335	340	14.70	14.20	13.70	13.30	12.80	12.30	11.80	11.40	10.90	10.40	10.00
340	345	15.00	14.60	14.10	13.60	13.10	12.70	12.20	11.70	11.20	10.80	10.30
345	350	15.40	14.90	14.40	14.00	13.50	13.00	12.50	12.10	11.60	11.10	10.60
350	355	15.70	15.20	14.80	14.30	13.80	13.40	12.90	12.40	11.90	11.50	11.00
355	360	16.10	15.60	15.10	14.60	14.20	13.70	13.20	12.70	12.30	11.80	11.30
360	365	16.40	15.90	15.50	15.00	14.50	14.00	13.60	13.10	12.60	12.10	11.70
365	370	16.80	16.30	15.80	15.30	14.90	14.40	13.90	13.40	13.00	12.50	12.00
370	375	17.10	16.60	16.10	15.70	15.20	14.70	14.30	13.80	13.30	12.80	12.40
375	380	17.50	17.00	16.50	16.00	15.50	15.10	14.60	14.10	13.70	13.20	12.70
380	385	17.90	17.40	16.90	16.40	15.90	15.40	14.90	14.50	14.00	13.50	13.10
385	390	18.20	17.70	17.20	16.70	16.20	15.80	15.30	14.80	14.30	13.90	13.40
390	395	18.60	18.10	17.60	17.10	16.60	16..10	15.60	15.20	14.70	14.20	13.70

* Taken from Wisconsin Tax Tables.

THEME

3

Tomorrow's Money: Getting to the End of the Rainbow

OVERVIEW

Have your parents told you that money doesn't grow on trees? This is good advice as far as it goes. Although money most definitely doesn't grow on trees, it can **grow**. It grows when you save and invest wisely. If you want to be wealthy, start by saving and investing regularly. Begin saving now and save as much as you can afford. Pay yourself first by putting money in a savings account or money market fund every time you are paid.

Because of the power of compounding, your money will grow *big time*. *Compounding* means that you earn interest on the interest earned in previous years. For example, if you save $2,000 and earn 8 percent annual interest, you will have $2,160 at the end of the first year. You earned $160 in interest. The second year, however, you will earn more than $160 in interest because you earn 8 percent of $2,160, not $2,000. This is $172.80 in interest, or $12.80 more than the first year.

So you earned $12.80 more the second year. Big deal. How much difference does this compounding make? If you save $2,000 a year at 8 percent annual interest from age 22 to age 65, you will have saved $86,000 over 43 years. How much money would you have at age 65? You would have a total of $713,899, or $627,899 more than you saved. Think of compound interest as the fertilizer that makes money grow. (Example from Dwight Lee and Richard McKenzie, *Getting Rich in America.*)

Financial Fitness for Life: Bringing Home the Gold Student Workouts, ©National Council on Economic Education

Of course, with a higher rate of return, money grows even faster. An 8 percent annual rate of return is not that difficult to achieve. The value of stocks has increased more than that, on average, over the last 60 years. If you earned 15 percent annual interest, your $86,000 would grow to $6,230,000 by the time you reach 65. Because of compounding, doubling the rate of return increases your stash of cash eight times. Obviously, the interest rate makes a huge difference.

But the people competing for your savings will not pay you a high interest rate out of kindness. Saving and investing will not only enrich you, but your investment dollars help businesses and the economy to grow. That's why banks, savings and loans, credit unions, governments, and companies pay you for the use of your money. *They* hope to gain by using *your* savings.

Some of these people competing for your savings will be taking more risks than others. They pay more to get you to take more risk. *Risk* is the chance that you might not get your money back. The higher the risk, the higher the potential reward. You might want to take some high risks with some of your savings but not with all of it. That is why you need to diversify your investments. *Diversification* means that you should not put all your eggs in one basket. Although diversification will not guarantee that your investments will not lose money, it should decrease the chance of that happening.

Money can work for you, but you will have to work to make it grow as much as possible, consistent with the risks you are willing to take. Investigate before you invest. There are millions of places you can invest, from very safe insured savings accounts to speculative stocks, commodity futures, and collectibles. A successful investor learns a lot about investing before making investment choices.

The lessons that follow will get you started, but you will never be able to stop learning if you want to invest successfully over your lifetime. There is a pot of gold at the end of that rainbow, but getting there takes hard work.

Questions

1. Why do people save and invest?

2. When is the best time to begin investing?

3. Why do savings grow so quickly?

4. Why do saving and investing help the overall economy?

5. What is the relationship between investment risk and reward?

6. What does it mean to diversify investments?

FAQs

ABOUT TOMORROW'S MONEY: GETTING TO THE END OF THE RAINBOW

1. Can most Americans become rich?

Yes. No matter what your income, regular saving and investing can make you rich. The key is to live below your means, save regularly, and find good investments. The earlier you start this, the richer you will become.

2. What is the difference between saving and investing?

The words, saving and investing, are used a lot in these lessons. Saving is putting money aside—not spending it now for goods and services. Individuals may place their money in savings accounts. These include passbook savings accounts and certificates of deposit that are insured by the Federal Deposit Insurance Corporation (FDIC). Investing generally is seen as putting saved money into stocks, corporate bonds, mutual funds, commercial real estate, and other financial instruments or ventures. Each of these investments carry more risk than savings accounts.

Don't be too concerned about the differences between savings and investing. We sometimes use these words interchangeably in these lessons.

3. Why shouldn't I just keep my money in a savings account where it will be safe?

This depends on your definition of "safe." The money is perfectly safe in an insured savings account, but what if the annual interest rate is less than the rate of inflation? With inflation, your money loses purchasing power. What if you save enough to buy a mountain bike, but when you take the money out, it buys only half a bike? That's why some people put money in riskier, long-term investments that can provide a greater return—one where the purchasing power of your savings/investment keeps pace with or exceeds inflation.

4. What is the difference between investing and gambling?

Some people say that purchasing stocks or mutual funds is the same as buying a lottery ticket, betting on a sporting event, or playing the slot machines. Gambling and investing both involve risk, but there are big differences. Gambling involves random chance and is what economists call a "zero-sum game." In other words, for every winner, there is a loser. It is a win-lose deal. Investing is not random and is a positive-sum game. Informed, deliberate choices increase your chances of making

FAQs

**ABOUT GETTING TO THE END
OF THE RAINBOW**
continued

money on your investments. A positive-sum game is an activity involving more than one person in which one person can gain without reducing another person's gain. It is a win-win deal. For example, the Standard & Poor's 500 Stock Index increased at a compounded annual rate of 12.7 percent from 1926 to 1997. This means a lot of people made money and no one had to lose money. It was a win for long-term investors.

5. Are good investments hard to find?

The problem is not finding good investments but evaluating them. For example, there are thousands of stocks traded on the New York Stock Exchange, Nasdaq, and the American Stock Exchange. Over 9,000 mutual funds fall into 33 broad categories. The federal, state, and local governments and corporations sell bonds. Thousands of banks, savings and loans, and credit unions offer all kinds of investment options.

6. Is there a secret to good investing?

There is no secret, but a few basic rules help:

- *Live below your means.*

- *Save early and often.*

- *Take prudent risks to achieve higher returns. Remember that the stock market has beaten the returns on every other type of investment over the long term.*

Financial Fitness for Life: Bringing Home the Gold Student Workouts, ©National Council on Economic Education

EXERCISE 8.1

The Opportunity Cost and Benefit of Spending and Saving

A person's income represents his or her scarce resources. Because resources are scarce, every decision involves an opportunity cost. The **opportunity cost** is what you give up to have something. The opportunity cost is the most valued option that you refused because you chose something else. The opportunity cost is your next best option.

One important choice everyone faces is whether to consume goods and services today or to consume goods and services later. Spending today brings immediate benefits or gratification. The opportunity cost is that you will have less money to buy goods and services in the future. Saving builds wealth to buy goods and services such as a car, house, or vacation in the future. The opportunity cost is not buying as many goods and services today.

Questions

1. What are the benefit and opportunity cost of spending your income today?

2. What are the benefit and opportunity cost of saving some of your income?

A Tale of Two Savers

The following case study is about two people who saved. Each earned 10 percent interest. Of course, the interest or rate of return for any one year can differ greatly.

Ana Gutierrez started saving when she was 22, right out of college. Saving involves an opportunity cost—the best alternative given up. It wasn't easy to save $2,000 a year then, considering her car loan, car, and rent payments. But Ana was determined to save because her grandmother always said it wasn't what you make but what you save that determines your wealth. So, reluctantly, Ana gave up buying that new car and renting a really nice apartment, and she saved $2,000 a year. After 12 years, she got tired of the sacrifice, yearning for a brand new red sports car and other luxuries. She didn't touch the money she had already saved because she wanted to be sure she would have money for retirement, which she planned to do at the end of her 65th year. But she quit saving and hit the stores.

Shawn Wright didn't start saving until he was 34. He also graduated from college at 22, but he had done without many things in college, and, now that he had an income, he wanted some of those things. He bought a new car and a very nice wardrobe and took some wonderful trips. But spending his current income involved an opportunity cost. By the time he was 34, Shawn was married, had many responsibilities, and decided he'd better start saving and planning for his financial future. He had also heard that it isn't what you have earned, but what you have saved, that determines your wealth. He figured he had 25 to 30 productive years left in his career. So, with new determination, Shawn saved $2,000 a year for the next 32 years until he retired at the end of his 65th year.

Which person do you believe had more savings at the end of his/her 65th year?

Now let's see what really happened. Using Table 8.1, "The Growth of Ana's and Shawn's Savings," answer the questions on the next page.

Questions

1. How much money had Ana put into savings by age 65?

2. How much money had Shawn put into savings by age 65?

3. How much savings (total wealth) did Ana have at the end of her 65th year?

4. How much savings (total wealth) did Shawn have at the end of his 65th year?

5. In money terms, what were the opportunity cost and benefit for Ana?

6. In money terms, what were the opportunity cost and benefit for Shawn?

7. What is as important as the amount saved and amount of time? Why?

8. What are the incentives for saving early?

9. What might be an opportunity cost for saving early?

10. What conclusions can you draw from this activity?

Financial Fitness for Life: Bringing Home the Gold Student Workouts, ©National Council on Economic Education

TABLE 8.1

The Growth of Ana's and Shawn's Savings

Age	Interest rate	Ana Gutierrez			Shawn Wright		
		Saved	Interest earned	Total saved at the end of year	Saved	Interest earned	Total saved at the end of year
21	10%	$0.00	$0.00	$0.00	$0.00	$0.00	$0.00
22	10%	$2,000.00	$200.00	$2,200.00	$0.00	$0.00	$0.00
23	10%	$2,000.00	$420.00	$4,620.00	$0.00	$0.00	$0.00
24	10%	$2,000.00	$662.00	$7,282.00	$0.00	$0.00	$0.00
25	10%	$2,000.00	$928.20	$10,210.20	$0.00	$0.00	$0.00
26	10%	$2,000.00	$1,221.02	$13,431.22	$0.00	$0.00	$0.00
27	10%	$2,000.00	$1,543.12	$16,974.34	$0.00	$0.00	$0.00
28	10%	$2,000.00	$1,897.43	$20,871.78	$0.00	$0.00	$0.00
29	10%	$2,000.00	$2,287.18	$25,158.95	$0.00	$0.00	$0.00
30	10%	$2,000.00	$2,715.90	$29,874.85	$0.00	$0.00	$0.00
31	10%	$2,000.00	$3,187.48	$35,062.33	$0.00	$0.00	$0.00
32	10%	$2,000.00	$3,706.23	$40,768.57	$0.00	$0.00	$0.00
33	10%	$2,000.00	$4,276.86	$47,045.42	$0.00	$0.00	$0.00
34	10%	$0.00	$4,704.54	$51,749.97	$2,000.00	$200.00	$2,200.00
35	10%	$0.00	$5,175.00	$56,924.96	$2,000.00	$420.00	$4,620.00
36	10%	$0.00	$5,692.50	$62,617.46	$2,000.00	$662.00	$7,282.00
37	10%	$0.00	$6,261.75	$68,879.21	$2,000.00	$928.20	$10,210.20
38	10%	$0.00	$6,887.92	$75,767.13	$2,000.00	$1,221.02	$13,431.22
39	10%	$0.00	$7,576.71	$83,343.84	$2,000.00	$1,543.12	$16,974.34
40	10%	$0.00	$8,334.38	$91,678.22	$2,000.00	$1,897.43	$20,871.78
41	10%	$0.00	$9,167.82	$100,846.05	$2,000.00	$2,287.18	$25,158.95
42	10%	$0.00	$10,084.60	$110,930.65	$2,000.00	$2,715.90	$29,874.85
43	10%	$0.00	$11,093.06	$122,023.71	$2,000.00	$3,187.48	$35,062.33
44	10%	$0.00	$12,202.37	$134,226.09	$2,000.00	$3,706.23	$40,768.57
45	10%	$0.00	$13,422.61	$147,648.69	$2,000.00	$4,276.86	$47,045.42
46	10%	$0.00	$14,764.87	$162,413.56	$2,000.00	$4,904.54	$53,949.97
47	10%	$0.00	$16,241.36	$178,654.92	$2,000.00	$5,595.00	$61,544.96
48	10%	$0.00	$17,865.49	$196,520.41	$2,000.00	$6,354.50	$69,899.46
49	10%	$0.00	$19,652.04	$216,172.45	$2,000.00	$7,189.95	$79,089.41
50	10%	$0.00	$21,617.25	$237,789.70	$2,000.00	$8,108.94	$89,198.35
51	10%	$0.00	$23,778.97	$261,568.67	$2,000.00	$9,119.83	$100,318.18
52	10%	$0.00	$26,156.87	$287,725.54	$2,000.00	$10,231.82	$112,550.00
53	10%	$0.00	$28,772.55	$316,498.09	$2,000.00	$11,455.00	$126,005.00
54	10%	$0.00	$31,649.81	$348,147.90	$2,000.00	$12,800.50	$140,805.50
55	10%	$0.00	$34,814.79	$382,962.69	$2,000.00	$14,280.55	$157,086.05
56	10%	$0.00	$38,296.27	$421,258.96	$2,000.00	$15,908.60	$174,994.65
57	10%	$0.00	$42,125.90	$463,384.85	$2,000.00	$17,699.47	$194,694.12
58	10%	$0.00	$46,338.49	$509,723.34	$2,000.00	$19,669.41	$216,363.53
59	10%	$0.00	$50,972.33	$560,695.67	$2,000.00	$21,836.35	$240,199.88
60	10%	$0.00	$56,069.57	$616,765.24	$2,000.00	$24,219.99	$266,419.87
61	10%	$0.00	$61,676.52	$678,441.76	$2,000.00	$26,841.99	$295,261.86
62	10%	$0.00	$67,844.18	$746,285.94	$2,000.00	$29,726.19	$326,988.05
63	10%	$0.00	$74,628.59	$820,914.53	$2,000.00	$32,898.80	$361,886.85
64	10%	$0.00	$82,091.45	$903,005.99	$2,000.00	$36,388.68	$400,275.53
65	10%	$0.00	$90,300.60	$993,306.59	$2,000.00	$40,227.55	$442,503.09

Why It Pays to Save Early and Often

Suppose you put $1,000 into an investment that earns 10 percent interest. You leave it there for 10 years. You might expect to have earnings of $1,000 or a total of $2,000 in your account ($1,000 x .1 x 10 = $1,000). Adding the $1,000 in earnings to your original $1,000, you would have $2,000, right?

Wrong! You would have more than that. The return will be much higher because you earn interest not just on the principal but also on the interest you have already earned. This is called compound interest.

Here's how compounding works. Let's assume that 10 percent interest is compounded annually. This first year you earn $100 in interest. Now you have $1,100. The second year you earn interest on $1,100 ($1,100 x .1 = $110).

Because of compound interest, you can find out how long money will take to double by dividing 72 by the interest rate or the rate of return. With the rule of 72, you can calculate how long it will take your money to double at a certain interest rate as long as you don't spend the earnings. For example, at 10 percent interest, money will double in 7.2 years if the interest is compounded (72 ÷ 10 = 7.2 years).

Let's see how long it will take money to double.

Investment	Interest or rate of return	Years to double
Passbook savings	3%	_____
Money market account	6%	_____
U.S. Treasury Bond	7%	_____
Stock market	12%	_____

Because of compounding, it pays to save early and often. Early opportunity costs can bring large benefits. The factors that affect how much savings grow are:

- The earlier or longer you save, the more savings you will have.

- The more income you save each year, the more savings you will have.

- The higher the interest rate or rate of return, the more savings you will have.

Question

1. One key point in the economic way of thinking is that people respond to incentives. What is the incentive for saving early and often?

Types of Investment Risk

People save and invest their money to receive a return on that saving or investment. In this lesson, we will call any type of saving or investing an "investment." The **return** is the income earned. That return is stated as a percentage of the amount invested; it is usually calculated on a yearly or annual basis. Then it is called the **rate of return.**

Risk is the uncertainty that you will receive the promised return. The greater the risk you take with your investment, the higher the potential rate of return and the greater the chance that you might not receive that return. In other words, you are paid for the risk you take with your money. As with any economic decision, there is no free lunch in deciding about investments. Here are some of the risks you take when you invest your money.

FINANCIAL RISK

Financial risk is the risk that the business or government will not be able to return your money —much less pay a rate of return. Businesses, state agencies, and local governments have on some occasions declared bankruptcy. The U.S. government prints money, so there is no financial risk that it will not pay off its bonds. Insured savings accounts are insured up to $100,000 by an agency of the federal government, so they carry very little financial risk.

MARKET PRICE RISK

This is the risk that the price of an investment will go down. This rarely happens to money saved in a bank, savings and loan, or credit union. However, the prices of stocks, bonds, and mutual funds are determined by supply and demand, and they do go down (as well as up).

The *supply* of an investment is the different quantities of that investment that will be offered for sale at various prices during a specific time period. The *demand* for an investment refers to the different quantities of an investment that will be purchased at various prices during a specific time period. The *equilibrium price* is the price at which buyers want to buy the same amount of an investment that sellers want to sell.

The important point is that anything that changes the behavior of buyers and sellers can change the price of an investment. For example, technology stocks have been "hot" at various times. Prices increased because more people wanted technology stocks at various price levels (demand increased). When investors became less interested in technology stocks, the average price fell because fewer people wanted technology stocks at every price level (demand decreased).

LIQUIDITY RISK

Liquidity is the ability to turn your money into cash or spendable funds, such as a checking account. Some investments are very liquid. For example, some savings accounts allow you to withdraw your money at any time without a penalty. Stocks listed on a stock exchange are very liquid; you can buy or sell them at any time. Real estate and collectibles, on the other hand, are not very liquid because it takes time for a seller to find a buyer. Although the Internet is speeding up this process, there is no guarantee that a buyer and seller can get together on price and other terms for real estate and collectibles.

INFLATION RISK

Money is invested today in order to spend it tomorrow. The goal is to receive the original investment back plus a return, so that you will be able to buy more in the future.

Inflation can decrease the value of your investment. When you save or invest, you are deferring your spending until a later time. If prices rise over that time, your money will not go as far. Therefore, investors are more interested in the real rate of return than the nominal rate of return. The *real rate of return* is the nominal rate of return minus the inflation rate. For example, let's say you put your money in a certificate of deposit at an 8 percent rate of return. The annual rate of inflation is 3 percent. Therefore, your real rate of return is 5% (8% - 3% = 5%). The longer the time period, the greater the inflation risk.

FRAUD RISK

Some investments are misrepresented. In these cases, information about the investment is designed to deceive investors. Anyone can print a fancy brochure, make promises on the telephone, or guarantee great returns on the the Internet. Criminals often make up facts. Therefore, it is important to investigate before you invest. Most investment fraud occurs in securities and savings schemes that do not involve banks, savings and loans, credit unions, and brokerage firms.

Questions

1. What is the annual rate of return on an investment?

2. If you earn $40 a year on a $500 investment, what is the annual rate of return?

3. What is the relationship between the expected rate of return and the investment risk?

4. If the annual nominal rate of return on an investment is 10 percent and the annual rate of inflation is 3 percent, what is the real rate of return?

5. True, false, or uncertain and why? "The Internet is the future of our economy. The prices of Internet stocks are bound to go up."

6. True, false, or uncertain and why? "This investment pays 30 percent a year and is perfectly safe. I put my mother's money into this investment."

The Pyramid of Risk and Reward

**Highest Risk/
Highest Potential Return or Loss**

Speculative Stocks

Real Estate

Individual Stocks

Stock Mutual Funds

Money Market Mutual Funds

Insured Certificates of Deposit

Insured Savings Accounts

U.S. Savings Bond

U.S. Government Securities

**Lowest Risk/
Lowest Potential Return or Loss**

The list above ranks investments according to their risks and rewards. The higher an investment is on the pyramid, the greater the risk. Because the risk is greater, the potential rewards and potential losses are greater.

Your job is to rank each of these investments on a 1-3 scale with 3 representing the most risk or reward. Circle the number that best represents each risk or reward. For risk, "1" is the lowest risk and "3" the highest risk. For reward, "1" is the lowest reward and "3" the highest reward. Give reasons for your rank of each of the risks and reward. Let's go for it.

61

EXERCISE 9.2 Continued

MATTRESS

You could hide your money under a mattress.

Financial Risk	1	2	3
Market Price Risk	1	2	3
Liquidity Risk	1	2	3
Inflation Risk	1	2	3
Reward	1	2	3

Why?

REGULAR (PASSBOOK) SAVINGS ACCOUNT

The Federal Deposit Insurance Corporation (FDIC) insures savings accounts for up to $100,000. Interest rates are usually lower than rates for other types of savings choices, but you can open an account with very little money. You can also withdraw your money whenever you like.

Financial Risk	1	2	3
Market Price Risk	1	2	3
Liquidity Risk	1	2	3
Inflation Risk	1	2	3
Reward	1	2	3

Why?

CERTIFICATE OF DEPOSIT

CDs are a special type of savings deposit that you must leave in the bank for a set amount of time during which you receive a fixed rate of interest. The FDIC also insures these accounts for up to $100,000. Banks usually require that you deposit at least $500. If you withdraw your money before the end of the given time, you must pay a penalty.

Financial Risk	1	2	3
Market Price Risk	1	2	3
Liquidity Risk	1	2	3
Inflation Risk	1	2	3
Reward	1	2	3

Why?

MONEY MARKET MUTUAL FUNDS

These funds are sold by companies that sell stocks, bonds, and other types of investments. The fund's managers lend money to businesses and governments for short periods of time. For every dollar put in such a fund, an investor can expect to get back a dollar plus interest. Although money market mutual funds are not insured by the federal government, they are low-risk investments. Interest rates are usually higher than on bank accounts but lower than for stocks and bonds bought and held for the long term. Investors can get their money at any time; they can even write checks on the account.

Financial Risk	1	2	3
Market Price Risk	1	2	3
Liquidity Risk	1	2	3
Inflation Risk	1	2	3
Reward	1	2	3

Why?

STOCKS

Stocks are shares of ownership in a corporation. When you buy stock, you usually take a greater risk than you would with any other type of investing. Your reward will vary, depending on the prices you pay for your stocks and the dividends you receive. Stock on exchanges such as the New York Stock Exchange and Nasdaq can be bought and sold any time the exchange is open. The amount of money you need to buy stock depends on the prices of the stocks you want to buy and the number of shares you want.

Financial Risk	1	2	3
Market Price Risk	1	2	3
Liquidity Risk	1	2	3
Inflation Risk	1	2	3
Reward	1	2	3

Why?

U.S. GOVERNMENT SAVINGS BONDS

You can buy savings bonds from the federal government for as little as $50. You can't sell them to other people, but you can sell them to the government whenever you want cash. There are limits on when you can sell them before maturity without a penalty of loss of interest.

Financial Risk	1	2	3
Market Price Risk	1	2	3
Liquidity Risk	1	2	3
Inflation Risk	1	2	3
Reward	1	2	3

Why?

63

EXERCISE 9.2 Continued

STOCK MUTUAL FUNDS

Stock mutual funds invest in stocks. The risk depends on the investment objective. Some funds invest in high quality or blue-chip stocks, and others invest in more speculative stocks. The major difference in buying a fund rather than individual stocks is that you own many stocks, and you don't have all your eggs in one basket. Therefore, the risk is lower than with an individual stock. You can sell your shares in the fund back to the fund company at any time.

Financial Risk	1	2	3
Market Price Risk	1	2	3
Liquidity Risk	1	2	3
Inflation Risk	1	2	3
Reward	1	2	3

Why?

REAL ESTATE

Most investors in real estate buy the house they live in. Houses can increase in value, but housing prices can also fall. Sometimes when they rise, they rise less than the inflation rate. To sell your house, you must find a buyer. Many buyers and sellers use real estate brokers.

Financial Risk	1	2	3
Market Price Risk	1	2	3
Liquidity Risk	1	2	3
Inflation Risk	1	2	3
Reward	1	2	3

Why?

Financial Fitness for Life: Bringing Home the Gold Student Workouts, ©National Council on Economic Education

Investment Bingo

There are 24 terms below the bingo board. Write one term in each square so that you have 24 different terms on your board.

		Free Lunch		

Rate of return	Compound Interest	Opportunity cost
Incentive	Income	Wealth/Net worth
Rule of 72	Financial risk	Market price risk
Liquidity risk	Real rate of return	Fraud risk
Nominal rate of return	Passbook savings account	U.S. Savings Bond
Certificate of deposit	Inflation	Inflation risk
Money market mutual fund	Stock mutual fund	Stocks
Real estate	Annual rate of return	Risk/Reward ratiom

THEME 4

Spending and Credit Are Serious Business

OVERVIEW

Just about every adult in America uses credit. In 1999, 78 million households in the United States had a credit card. Yet, some people are afraid of using credit. "Neither a lender nor a borrower be" is an old adage such people might quote. Other people are fearless about using credit. They might say, "Hey, it's only plastic! Let's go for it!"

There are problems with both viewpoints. Used in a smart way, credit can be a tremendous help to you now and in the future. Used in a stupid way, credit can result in harassment, broken relationships, and bankruptcy.

What is credit? Credit means obtaining the use of money that you do not have. Obtaining credit means convincing someone else (a financial institution like a bank, savings and loan, credit union, or a credit card company) to voluntarily provide a loan to you in return for a promise to pay it back later plus an additional charge called interest.

Can using credit help you? You bet! Using credit allows you to use a good or a service today and pay for it later. Using credit can help people acquire valuable assets (like a college education or a home). Credit can also add to the enjoyment of life.

Can using credit hurt you? You bet! Loans have to be repaid. Lenders charge interest for the use of their money. Individuals have to sacrifice things they

Financial Fitness for Life: Bringing Home the Gold Student Workouts, ©National Council on Economic Education

wish to have today because they are required to pay for goods or services they have already consumed.

So, the key is to be smart about the use of credit.

What do lenders look for when they approve a loan to an individual? Ordinarily, they look for the "Three Cs":

✔ **Character:** Will the applicant be responsible and repay the loan?

✔ **Capacity:** Does the applicant have enough discretionary income to comfortably make the payments on the loan amount requested?

✔ **Collateral:** Will the loan be secured, or guaranteed, by collateral that can be used to repay the debt in case the borrower defaults on the loan?

Consumers sometimes make mistakes in using credit. They are not perfect. People in the lending business also make mistakes. They are not perfect either. The world of finance can be complicated. Some business people take advantage of consumers. Several state and federal laws are designed to protect credit consumers from dishonest business practices. Among the more important consumer credit protection laws are the Truth in Lending Act and the Fair Credit Reporting Act.

And then there are the scheme artists and swindlers. Unfortunately, the credit and finance industry sometimes attracts some unsavory sorts who prey on people's greed or financial fears. If you receive a phone call describing an investment that sounds too good to be true, it is. Hang up the phone. Avoid businesses that provide financial services but at very high costs—such as payday loans and rent-to-own plans.

Questions

1. What is credit?

2. What is an advantage to using credit?

3. What is a disadvantage to using credit?

4. What do lenders look for when they approve a loan to an individual?

5. Do credit consumers have legal protections?

Financial Fitness for Life: Bringing Home the Gold Student Workouts, ©National Council on Economic Education

ABOUT SPENDING AND CREDIT ARE SERIOUS BUSINESS

1. What is APR?

APR is the annual percentage rate. An APR is the interest rate you pay in a single year on the money you borrow.

2. Should you shop for credit cards?

Shopping for credit cards can save you money. Credit cards differ in what they charge for annual fees and the APR. They also differ in the time you have to pay the credit card balance owed without being charged interest (grace period) and the maximum amount you can charge (the credit limit).

3. Obtaining a home mortgage can be complicated. How can I figure out what the payments are going to be?

*The amount of a loan payment for a big purchase like a home or a car has already been worked out for you. Use an amortization table to calculate the interest and the monthly payments. Visit the Mortgage Bankers Association at **www.mbaa.org/cgi-bin/calculators.asp** to check one out.*

4. What is the Truth in Lending Act?

The Truth in Lending Act requires that creditors disclose the cost of the credit in simple terms. The lender must state the percentage cost of borrowing in terms of the annual percentage rate (APR), which takes into account all the costs of financing. The Truth in Lending Act also protects against unauthorized use of credit cards.

5. What is the Fair Credit Reporting Act?

The Fair Credit Reporting Act governs the activities of credit bureaus and creditors. Among other things, the Fair Credit Reporting Act requires creditors to furnish accurate and complete information regarding your credit history.

6. What is a payday loan?

A payday loan allows a person to get cash until payday with no credit background check. It is a legal loan. The applicant signs an agreement, writes a postdated check, and gets the cash. The check is held until the loan is repaid—usually about two weeks. The lender then deposits the check. Typically, the interest rate (APR) is quite high. The APR may be 500 percent or higher. It is easy for people in financial trouble to fall behind in paying off a payday loan.

7. What is rent-to-own?

Rent-to-own companies rent and sell appliances, furniture, and electronics to consumers. It is a legal business. Typically, a consumer agrees to rent something for a short period—one week or a month. If the consumer rents the product for a specified period of time (often 18 months), the consumer will become the owner of the product either automatically or by making an additional payment. Purchasing merchandise from a rent-to-own company usually costs 2 to 5 times as much as purchasing the goods from a department store or appliance store.

68

What Is Credit?

Credit allows individuals to obtain the use of money that they do not have. Obtaining credit means convincing someone else (a lender) to voluntarily provide a loan in return for a promise to pay it back plus an additional charge called interest. People obtain loans to buy cars, homes, and major appliances, improve their homes, pay for college education, and so forth.

Credit decisions can be difficult. Like all difficult decisions, credit decisions involve examining the advantages and disadvantages facing the individual making the choice. The hard part, of course, is figuring out whether the advantages of using credit outweigh the disadvantages.

There is a bright side to using credit. Credit can help people acquire assets. Assets are goods or services that usually retain or increase in value. Ordinarily, a home or post-secondary education is considered an asset. Credit can help people lead happier lives by helping them to obtain the goods and services they wish to have while paying for them. Credit also can help people in an emergency.

There is also a dark side to using credit. Mistakes in using too much credit in relation to your income can be hard ones from which to recover. Many new college graduates, for example, spend a lot of the income from their first jobs repaying large credit card debts they have rolled up while in college. These repayments mean they have to spend a lot of their current income on previous purchases, leaving less money to buy things they currently want. Misusing credit—missing payments or defaulting on loans—has many negative consequences including the inability to get credit later for major purchases, such as homes and cars.

Financial institutions (commercial banks, savings and loans, credit unions, and consumer finance companies) hold money that they, in turn, loan out to others. The owners of financial institutions expect to be compensated when they make a loan. This compensation is called "interest." Interest is the price a borrower pays to a lender for use of the lender's deposits. Interest is the reward lenders receive for allowing others to use their deposits.

Both sides in a credit transaction almost always benefit. Borrowers are able to purchase something that may be of value today and perhaps in the future. Lenders are repaid the money that was loaned, plus interest.

An important factor in determining the rate of interest to be charged is the amount of confidence the lender has that the amount of the loan plus interest will be repaid in the agreed upon time. Higher risk loans—loans where it is uncertain that the borrower can repay—usually result in higher interest rates.

EXERCISE 11.1 Continued

Lower risk loans—loans where it seems evident that the borrower can repay—usually result in lower interest rates.

A loan for an intangible, like a vacation, is likely to cost more in interest than a loan for a tangible item, like a home. Loans that are backed by other assets (your car) are likely to have lower interest rates than loans that are not backed by other assets. An asset used to back a loan is called *collateral*.

Questions

1. What is credit?

2. What is the bright side of using credit?

3. What is the dark side of using credit?

4. What institutions are sources of credit?

5. What is interest?

6. Who most often wins in a credit transaction?

7. How does risk influence the rate of interest?

8. What is collateral?

Common Forms of Credit

Directions: Study the chart below and answer the questions that follow.

Type of Credit	Lender	Advantages	Disadvantages
HOME MORTGAGE	• Commercial bank • Savings and loan • Credit union	• Homes often increase in value. • Interest rates for mortgages are relatively low. • The interest paid is tax-deductible.	• Mortgages are long-term commitments. • Obtaining a home loan involves extensive credit checks.
CAR LOANS	• Commercial bank • Savings and loan • Credit union • Consumer finance company	• Cars can make it easier to work and earn an income.	• Cars lose their value relatively quickly. The car you purchase on credit may have little value when the last payment is made.
COLLEGE LOANS	• Commercial bank • Savings and loan • Credit union	• A college education is usually a good investment. • Interest rates can be relatively low.	• Students sometimes borrow more than necessary. • New graduates can face difficulty in repaying large loans.
PERSONAL LOANS	• Commercial bank • Savings and loan • Credit union • Consumer finance company	• Personal loans allow individuals to purchase today that boat or vacation they want.	• Personal loans have relatively high interest rates. • Some young people may borrow more than their income should allow.
CREDIT CARDS	• Commercial bank • Savings and loan • Department store • Oil companies • Other financial institutions, e.g., American Express	• Credit cards are convenient to use and useful in an emergency. • Credit cards provide a record of charges.	• Credit cards have relatively high interest rates. • Some young people may borrow more than their income should allow.

Questions

1. What are the advantages of home loans and college loans compared to credit card and personal loans?

2. What are the disadvantages of credit card and college loans?

Financial Fitness for Life: Bringing Home the Gold Student Workouts, ©National Council on Economic Education

Credit Research

Directions: Contact by phone, in person, or on the Internet each of the following financial institutions in your community. Ask what the current annual percentage rate (APR) is for each of the loans listed. The APR is the commonly used way in which interest rates are expressed. Record the information in the correct places on the chart and share the results in class.

Credit Research Results

Loan ▶ Institution ▼	APR for a car loan	APR for a college loan	APR for a home mortgage	APR for a credit card	APR for a loan for a vacation
Commercial Bank					
Savings and Loan					
Credit Union					
Consumer Finance Company					

Questions

1. Which local institutions offered the best APR for each type of loan?

2. Which local institutions offered the highest APR for each type of loan?

Fickle Financial Advisors

Part I YOUR JOB

You run a small consulting business giving advice to people who are thinking about applying for credit. For a small fee, you offer your customers advice on whether they should apply for a loan. Your business has been successful because you understand clearly the advantages and disadvantages of using various forms of credit. You ask what is most important to the future success of your clients, and you compare the risks of using credit to the benefits using credit can offer.

Advantages to using credit:

- Credit can help people acquire valuable assets.
- Credit can help people lead happier lives.
- Credit can help people in an emergency.

Disadvantages to using credit:

- People may use too much credit in relation to their income.
- Misusing credit can lead to paying more to obtain credit in the future.
- Misusing credit can hurt the ability of people to obtain credit in the future.

After reading each client's case, ask yourself:

 Questions

1. Is the loan being used to purchase a valuable asset?

2. Do you think the client is likely to be able to repay the loan?

Some people may think that making credit recommendations based on these two questions is too restrictive — a real killjoy attitude. They may be right. Nevertheless, your company has helped many clients to understand how the careful use of credit can result in improving overall personal wealth.

73

EXERCISE 12.1 Continued

Part II THE CLIENTS

Client 1

I am 17 years old and a high school senior. I have earned good grades in high school. I have been admitted to a good state university. I would like to go to college full-time and work only a few hours a week. With this schedule, I think that I can complete my college degree in four years. I am planning to major in chemical engineering. My college advisor has told me that chemical engineering is a hard major. My parents have no money to support me in college. I am planning to use college loans to pay for my college tuition and books. I plan to live at home and work in the summer to earn spending money for use during the school year. I will be borrowing about $25,000. Should I apply for the loan?

1. What is the main advantage of getting credit?

2. What is the main disadvantage of getting credit?

3. Do you recommend that this client apply for the loan? Explain.

Client 2

I am 18 years old. I attend the local vocational-technical school. My area of study is commercial heating and cooling. My school tuition is relatively low and the program only takes nine months. I can pay most of my expenses by working full time in the summer and part time during the school year. I am still living at home, and I plan to get an apartment of my own next year. I am an avid sports fan. I have a little 12-inch television set in my room. I'd like to use my credit card to buy a really big 38-inch television set at a cost of $1,500.

1. What is the main advantage of getting credit?

2. What is the main disadvantage of getting credit?

3. Do you recommend that this client apply for the loan? Explain.

Client 3

I am 21 years old and finishing my last year in college. I have been studying hard and have earned relatively good grades. My major is English. A small group of my friends want to bust out for spring break and take a one-week vacation in Florida. I have never really had a vacation while in college except for two trips with my family. If I book my reservations now, I can get relatively low air fare and hotel rates. I am a little low on cash. I am planning to charge the $1,500 for the trip on my credit card.

1. What is the main advantage of getting credit?

2. What is the main disadvantage of getting credit?

3. Do you recommend that this client apply for the loan? Explain.

Client 4

I am 22 years old. I am just about to complete a two-year dental hygienist program at a local vocational school. My first-year pay will be about $25,000 plus fringe benefits including health insurance and a 401k program. My workplace is 20 miles from my apartment and is not on a city bus route. The car I have has 225,000 miles on the odometer, and it burns more oil than gas. Yesterday, I noticed that I can see the road through a hole in the floor in front of the driver's seat! I have saved up $2,000 for a down payment on a new car, but I will need to borrow several thousand more to buy a new but small and dependable car.

1. What is the main advantage of getting credit?

2. What is the main disadvantage of getting credit?

3. Do you recommend that this client apply for the loan? Explain.

Financial Fitness for Life: Bringing Home the Gold Student Workouts, ©National Council on Economic Education

Reading a Credit Report

Your ability to qualify for a loan depends on a credit report. A credit report is a record of an individual's personal credit history. It is probably a good indicator of the applicant's character and whether he or she will repay the money as agreed.

When a person applies for a loan, the lender will order a credit report to see how well the applicant has managed credit in the past. A credit report will tell, in detail, how much the person has borrowed, from whom, and whether the bills have been paid on time.

Credit reports are compiled by credit bureaus, which regularly collect information on millions of consumers. Credit bureaus get information from a variety of sources, including stores, credit card companies, banks, mortgage companies, and medical providers. When you fill out an application for credit, the information on that application is also sent to a credit bureau.

WHAT ARE CREDITORS LOOKING FOR?

Lenders look for certain qualities in loan applicants. These qualities are called the Three Cs of Credit: *capacity, character,* and *collateral*. A discussion of each follows.

Capacity: The credit application will contain questions that refer to the ability of the consumer to repay the debt. The basic question is: "Have you been working regularly in an occupation that is likely to provide enough income to support your use of credit?" More particular questions might address the following:

- ✔ Do you have a steady job?
- ✔ What is your salary?
- ✔ How reliable is your income?
- ✔ Do you have other sources of income?
- ✔ How many other loan payments do you have?
- ✔ What are your current living expenses?
- ✔ What are your current debts?
- ✔ How many dependents do you have?
- ✔ Do you pay alimony or child support?
- ✔ Can you afford your lifestyle?

Character: Questions will be asked to determine whether you possess the honesty and reliability to pay credit debts. Here are some examples:

✔ Have you used credit before?

✔ Do you pay your bills on time?

✔ Do you have a good credit report?

✔ Can you provide character references?

✔ How long have you lived at your present address?

✔ How long have you been at your present job?

Collateral: Collateral serves as a type of insurance for the creditor. The creditor is interested in determining whether you have any assets that could be sold to pay off your loan in the event that you are unable to do so. Questions may include the following:

✔ Do you have a checking account?

✔ Do you have a savings account?

✔ Do you own any stocks or bonds?

✔ Do you have any valuable collections or jewelry?

✔ Do you own your own home?

✔ Do you own a car?

✔ Do you own a boat?

THE IMPORTANCE OF A GOOD CREDIT RATING

A *good* rating on a credit report means that in the past bills have been paid on time. A *poor* rating indicates overdue or unpaid items.

It is extremely important to build and maintain a good credit history. A good credit report can often make the difference between getting a loan or being turned down. In addition, potential employers and landlords will often check an applicant's credit report before making a final decision about offering a job or a rental.

CREDIT REPORTS MAY CONTAIN ERRORS

Mistakes can and do occur on credit reports. For example, a credit report may contain information about someone with the same name, or paid accounts may be listed as unpaid. The law provides individuals with a means of requesting and reviewing their credit report and having mistakes corrected. Under the Fair Credit Reporting Act you have the right to get a copy of your credit report from a credit bureau. The three largest credit bureaus in 2001 are:

✔ Equifax

✔ Experian

✔ Trans Union

EXERCISE 13.1 Continued

WAYS TO ESTABLISH AND KEEP A GOOD CREDIT HISTORY

There are several steps you can take to establish and maintain a good credit history.

- ✔ Always pay your bills on time.
- ✔ Never borrow more than you can comfortably pay back.
- ✔ Borrow only the amount you need.
- ✔ Know how much you owe at all times.
- ✔ Contact lenders immediately if you expect to have a payment problem.
- ✔ Develop good savings habits to handle financial emergencies without borrowing.
- ✔ Report lost or stolen credit cards immediately.
- ✔ Never give your credit card number over the phone unless you initiated the call.
- ✔ Open a checking account and a savings account.
- ✔ Do not apply for too many credit cards. Even if you don't use them, the credit limits are taken into consideration when you apply for credit.

Evaluating a Credit Report

Instructions: Study the credit report in Illustration 13.1 to answer the questions that follow.

Questions

1. Whose credit report is this?

2. How many potentially negative items are listed?

3. How many accounts are in good standing?

4. On page 2, there are two very negative items. What are they?

    a.

    b.

5. Have any of John Q. Consumer's credit cards been lost or stolen?

6. Does John Q. Consumer have a good credit record with First Credit Union and National Credit Card?

    What are the reasons for your opinion?

7. Who requested John Q. Consumer's credit report in 1999?

    a.

    b.

    c.

8. Is John Q. Consumer a homeowner?

9. What is the most negative item on this report, and for how many years does that item stay on the credit report?

10. If you were a lender, would you grant John Q. Consumer credit? Why or why not?

ILLUSTRATION
13.1

Credit Report of John Q. Consumer

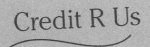

Prepared for	**Report date**
JOHN Q. CONSUMER	June 01, 1999
Report number	
1687771839-0000051088	**Page 1 of 8**

Credit R Us
P.O. Box 9595
Allen TX 75013-9595

Personal Credit Report

About this report

Credit R Us collects and organizes information about you and your credit history from public records, your creditors and other reliable sources. We make your credit history available to your current and prospective creditors and employers as allowed by law. We do not grant credit or evaluate your credit history. Personal data about you may be made available to companies whose products and services interest you.

Important decisions about your creditworthiness are based on the information in this report. You should review it carefully for accuracy.

Report number

Below is a summary of the information contained in this report.

Potentially negative items listed   2

Public records   2
Accounts with creditors and others   3

Accounts in good standing   3

If you have questions
For all questions about this report, please call us at: **1-888-000-0000**
M - F 7:30am - 7 pm CT

To learn more about Credit R Us or for other helpful information, including tips on how to improve your creditworthiness, visit our web site:
http://www.creditrus.com

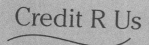

Prepared for	**Report date**
JOHN Q. CONSUMER	June 01, 1999
Report number	
1687771839-0000051088	**Page 2 of 8**

Information affecting your creditworthiness

Items listed with dashes before and after the number, *for example –1–*, may have a potentially negative effect on your future credit extension and are listed first on the report.

Credit grantors may carefully review the items listed below when they check your credit history. Please note that the account information connected with some public records, such as bankruptcy, also may appear with your credit accounts listed later in this report.

Important decisions about your creditworthiness are based on the information in this report. You should review it carefully for accuracy.

Your statement

At your request, we've included the following statement every time your credit report is requested.

"My identification has been used without my consent on applications for credit. Please call me at 999.999.9999 before approving credit in my name."

Public record information about you

Source/ Identification number	Location number	Date filed/ Date resolved	Responsibility	Claim amount/ Liability amount	Comments
-1- HOLLY COW DIST CT 305 MAIN STREET HOLLY NJ 08060	B312P7659	3-1997/ NA	Joint	$3,756/ NA	Status: civil claim judgement filed. Plaintiff: Dime Savings. This item is scheduled to continue on record until 3-2004. This item was verified on 8-1997 and remained unchanged.
-2- BROWN TOWN HALL 10 COURT STREET BROWN NJ 02809	BK443PG14	11-1997/ NA	Joint	$57,786/ NA	Status: chapter 7 bankruptcy discharged. This item is scheduled to continue on record until 11-2007. This item was verified on 8-1997 and remained unchanged.

80

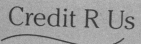

Credit R Us

Prepared for
JOHN Q. CONSUMER
Report number
1687771839-0000051088

Report date
June 01, 1999

Page 3 of 8

Credit information about you

Source/ Account number (except last few digits)	Date opened/ Reported since	Date of status/ Last reported	Type/ Terms/ Monthly payments	Responsibility	Credit limit or original amount/ High balance	Recent balance/ Recent payment	Comments
-3- FIDELITY BK NA 300 FIDELITY PLAZA NORTHSHORE NJ 08902 46576000024	6-1994/ 6-1994	12-1996/ 12-1996	Installment/ 10 months/ $0	Individual	$4,549/ NA	$4,549 as of 12-1996	Status: charge off.$4,549 written off in 12-1996. This account is scheduled to continue on until 12-2003
-4- B.B. CREDIT 35 WASHINGTON ST. DEDHAM MA 547631236	10-1990/ 4-1995	4-1998/ 4-1998	Installment/ 80 months/ $34	Individual	$8,500/ $8,500	$0 as of 4-1998/ $34	Status: Debt re-included in chapter 7 bankruptcy. $389 written off in 3-1998. Account history: Collection as of 9-1995 thru 6-1996 90 days as of 7-1995 60 days as of 11-1994, 6-1995 30 days as of 9-1994, 1-1995 and 2 other times This account is scheduled to continue on record until 2-2001. This item was verified and updated on 6-1996.

Credit R Us

Prepared for
JOHN Q. CONSUMER
Report number
1687771839-0000051088

Report date
June 01, 1999

Page 4 of 8

Credit information about you *continued*

Source/ Account number (except last few digits)	Date opened/ Reported since	Date of status/ Last reported	Type/ Terms/ Monthly payments	Responsibility	Credit limit or original amount/ High balance	Recent balance/ Recent payment	Comments
-5- FIRST CREDIT UNION 78 WASHINGTON LN LANEVILLE TX 76362 129474 Mortgage: 74848347834	3-1996/ 3-1996	11-1998/ 11-1998	Installment/ 48 Months/ $420		$17,856/ NA	$0 as of 11-1998/ $420	Status: open/never late.
-6- AMERICA FINANCE CORP PO BOX 8633 COLLEY IL 60126 6376001172....	6-1993/ 7-1993	11-1998/ 11-1998	Revolving/ NA/ $400		$0/ $18,251	$0 as of 11-1998	Status: card reported lost or stolen. This account is scheduled to continue on record until 11-2000.
-7- NATIONAL CREDIT CARD 100 THE PLAZA LANEVILLE NJ 08905 420000638....	6-1993/ 6-1993	11-1998/ 11-1998	Revolving/ NA/ $0	Joint with JANE CONSUMER	$8,000 $8,569	$0 as of 11-1998	Status: open/never late.

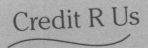

Prepared for
JOHN Q. CONSUMER

Report number
1687771839-0000051088

Report date
June 01, 1999

Page 5 of 8

Your use of credit

The information listed below provides **additional** detail about your accounts, showing up to 24 months of balance history and your credit limit, high balance or original loan amount. Not all balance history is reported to Credir R Us, so some of your accounts may not appear. Also, some credit grantors may update the information more than once in the same month.

Source/ Account number

Date/Balance

-6- AMERICA FINANCE CO. CORP.
6376001172

11-1998/$0   10-1998/$4,329   8-1998/$0   5-1998/$0   2-1998/$250   1-1998/$0   12-1997/$2,951
9-1997/$3,451   7-1997/$4,251   5-1997/$4,651   2-1997/$5,451   1-1997/$5,851;   12-1996/$6,251
11-1996/$6,651   9-1996/$7,051   7-1996/$7,451   5-1996/$7,852   3-1996/$8,251   1-1996/$12,651
12-1995/$9,051   11-1995/$9,451   9-1995/$10,251   7-1995/$10,651   5-1995/$11,051

Between 1-1994 and 11-1998 your credit limit was unknown.

-7- NATIONAL CREDIT CARD
420000638

11-1998/$0   9-1998/$542   7-1998/$300   6-1998/$686   4-1998/$1,400   3-1998/$2,500
1-1998/$2,774   12-1997/$599   9-1997/$873   7-1997/$1,413   5-1997/$1,765   4-1997/$2,387
3-1997/$3,400   2-1997/$3,212   1-1997/$4,412   12-1996/$2,453   10-1996/$2,453   10-1996/$1,769
8-1996/$1,200   4-1996/$3,200   2-1996/$4,568   1-1996/$5,582   12-1995/$3,000   10-1995/$3,200
8-1995/$4,500

Between 6-1993 and 11-1998 your credit limit was $8,000.

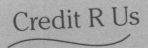

Prepared for
JOHN Q. CONSUMER

Report number
1687771839-0000051088

Report date
June 01, 1999

Page 6 of 8

Others who have requested your credit history

Listed below are all those who have received information from us in the recent past about your credit history.

Requests initiated by you

You took actions, such as completing a credit application, that allowed the following sources to review your information. Please note that the following information is part of your credit history and is included in our reports to others.

Source	Date	Comments
ABC MORTGAGE 64 MAPLE ROSEVILLE MD 02849	10-18-1998	Real estate loan of $214,000 on behalf of State Bank with 30 year repayment terms. This inquiry is scheduled to continue on record until 10-2000.

Other requests

You may not have initiated the following requests for your credit history, so you may not recognize each source. We offer credit information about you to those with a permissible purpose, for example, to:

- other creditors who want to offer you pre-approved credit;
- an employer who wishes to extend an offer of employment
- a potential investor in assessing the risk of a current obligation;
- Credit R Us Customers Assistance to process a report for you;
- your current creditors to monitor your accounts (date listed may affect only the most recent request).

We report these requests **only** to you as a record of activities, and we do not include **any** of these requests on credit reports to others.

Source	Date
CREDIT R US PO BOX 949 ALLEN TX 75013	3-99
WORLD BANK PO BOX 949 ALLEN TX 75013	3-99, 12-98, 9-98, 6-98, 3-98, 12-97, 9-97, 6-97, 3-97
FIDELITY BK NA 300 FIDELITY PLAZA NORTHSHORE NJ 08902	1-99, 7-98, 1-98, 7-97, 1-97
NATIONAL CREDIT REPORT 100 THE PLAZA LANEVILLE NJ 08905	7-97, 2-97

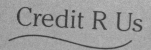

Prepared for
JOHN Q. CONSUMER
Report number
1687771839-0000051088

Report date
June 01, 1999

Page 7 of 8

Personal information about you

The following information associated with your records **has been reported to us by you, your creditors and other sources.** As part of our fraud-prevention program, a notice with additional information may appear in your report.

Names
JOHN Q. CONSUMER

Residences

Our records show you currently are a homeowner. The geographical code shown with each address identifies the state, country, census tract, block group and Metropolitan Statistical Area associated with each address.

Address	Type of address	Geographical code
7972 PADDOCK CT LANEVILLE, TX 00000	Single Family	0-192053-3-0
1777 BEVERLY AVE SOMEWHERE, NJ 00000	Single Family	0-224681-25-0
250 GARDEN DRIVE ANYWHERE, NJ 00000	Single Family	0-9004-93-0

Social Security numbers
000-00-0000
111-11-1111
222-22-2222

Year of birth
1954

Driver's license number
CA X123456

Spouses name
JANE

Driver's license number
CA X123456

Notices
The first Social Security number listed shows that credit was established before the number was issued.

Financial Fitness for Life: Bringing Home the Gold Student Workouts, ©National Council on Economic Education

EXERCISE 13.3

Evaluating Three Loan Applications

These are excerpts from the credit reports of three loan applicants. Based solely on their record of paying credit obligations in the past, decide whether you would approve or decline their loan requests. Check your response and then write the reason for that response.

Status codes given at the end of the reports.

JANICE BROWN	☐ APPROVE	☐ DECLINE	☐ NOT SURE	WHY?		
Company name	Months reviewed	High credit	Terms	Balance	Past due	Status
Sears	2	2,016	24	838		R3
Dept. of Educ.	7	1,507		1,507	158	I5
Dept. of Educ.	2	512		512	512	I5
ABC Credit Card	8	3,000	29	1363		R1
Record of Month	6			38	38	O3

Prior paying history: 30(01)60(02)90+(04)   8/94-I5   5/94-R4   8/94-I8

TITO SANDERS	☐ APPROVE	☐ DECLINE	☐ NOT SURE	WHY?		
Company name	Months reviewed	High credit	Terms	Balance	Past due	Status
Bank of America	24	11,000	60	5,350		I1
ABC Credit Card	6	2,500	36	0		O0
Dept. of Educ.	5	2,000	24	1,380		I1
XYZ Credit Card	12	3,000	24	495		R1

Prior paying history: 30(00)60(00)90+(00)

MARIA MARTINEZ	☐ APPROVE		☐ DECLINE	☐ NOT SURE	WHY?	
Company name	Months reviewed	High credit	Terms	Balance	Past due	Status
Bank of America	13	7,200	48	5,800		I1
ABC Credit Card	7	2,000	24	488		R1

Prior paying history: 30(01)60(00)90+(02) 3/94 I8 4/95 R9 3/96 I9

STATUS CODES

Type of account
O = Open
R = Revolving
I = Installment

Timeliness of payment
0 = Approved, not used
1 = Paid as agreed
2 = 30 days past due
3 = 60 days past due
4 = 90 days past due
5 = 120 days past due or collection account
7 = Making regular payments under wage earner plan
8 = Repossession
9 = Seriously delinquent/bad debt (paid or unpaid; charged off account)

EXERCISE
14.1

Everything You Wanted to Know About Figuring Interest

Credit isn't free. The cost of credit is called **interest** or the **finance charge.** The finance charge may be stated in dollars or as a percentage of the loan. When stated as a percentage of the loan, it is called the **interest rate.**

The *Truth in Lending Law* makes comparing credit costs simple. This federal law requires that all lenders state their finance charges and interest rates in the same way. This rate is called the *annual percentage rate* or *APR.* An APR is the rate you pay in a single year on the money you borrow. The APR is based on the amount of money you still have to pay back, not the amount of the original loan. In credit language, it is based on the *declining balance* of your loan.

Every loan must also state the finance charge. The *finance charge* is the total dollar amount of interest you must pay on the loan. The amount you borrow is called the *principal* of the loan. You pay back the principal plus the finance charge. The finance charge depends on the APR and the length of the loan. The higher the APR and the longer the period of the loan, the higher the finance charge.

Save Money on Interest—Go Figure

By using your math skills, you can save big bucks on a loan. Let's find out how.

Part I FIGURING SIMPLE INTEREST

First, let's figure some finance charges. The basic formula for figuring out interest is:

$$I = PRT$$

I—Interest (Finance charge)
P—Principal
R—Rate (an add-on rate)
T—Time (in years)

In this formula, the rate is an add-on rate with one payment of principal. The principal (amount of loan) and the interest are paid in one lump sum at the maturity date (end of loan period). For example, if you borrowed $2,000 at a 12 percent add-on rate for two years, the interest would be $480 ($480 = $2,000 x .12 x 2). The amount of $2,480 (interest and principal) would be repaid at the end of two years. Now answer these questions:

Questions

1. Gabrielle Daily borrows $1,000 at a 6 percent add-on rate for one year. What is the finance charge?

2. Jesse Candelaria borrows $2,000 at a 10 percent add-on rate for three years. What is the finance charge?

3. Jessica Tate borrows $2,000 at a 10 percent add-on rate for two years. What is the finance charge?

4. Travis Whitaker borrows $2,000 at an 8 percent add-on rate for two years. What is the finance charge?

5. If you want to lower the finance charge, should you shop for a higher or lower interest rate?

Why?

6. If you want to lower the finance charge, should you pay back the loan more quickly or less quickly?

Why?

EXERCISE 14.1 Continued

Part II FIGURING MONTHLY PAYMENTS

Most loans are paid back on a monthly basis. Very few are paid back all at once at the maturity value of the loan. The monthly payment is the amount the borrower must pay the lender each month to pay back the loan. The monthly payment covers principal and interest. This is the formula for figuring the monthly payment:

$$MP = \frac{P + I}{N}$$

MP—Monthly payment

P—Principal of the loan

I—Interest (Figure it as you did in the problems above)

N—Number of months the loan is for

For example, you borrow $10,000 at an 8 percent add-on rate for four years.

P = $10,000

I = ($10,000 x .08 x 4) or $3200

$$MP = \frac{(\$10,000 + \$3200)}{48} \text{ or } \$275$$

Questions

1. David Kim borrows $8,000 at an 8 percent add-on rate for two years.

- What is the interest?

- What is the monthly payment?

2. Maria Torres borrows $8,000 at an 8 percent add-on rate for four years.

- What is the interest?

- What is the monthly payment?

3. If a borrower takes longer to pay back a loan, what happens to the monthly payment?

4. If a borrower takes longer to pay back a loan, what happens to the interest?

5. What are the costs and benefits of taking longer to pay off a loan?

Part III DETERMINING THE APR

In the past, lenders advertised interest rates in various ways. In some instances, people were paying higher rates than they thought because lenders were figuring the rates differently. Consumers had difficulty shopping for credit because of these variations in figuring rates.

Let's look at a couple of examples to illustrate what was being done. Suppose George secures a $1,200 loan at 10 percent add-on interest for one year that he would pay off (interest and principal) at the end of the year. At the end of the year, he would pay $1,320 to the lender ($1,200 principal with $120 interest). The interest rate that was advertised for this loan was 10 percent.

Now suppose that Sheila secured a $1,200 loan with 10 percent add-on interest paying $110 a month. She would be paying a total of $1,320 as well. Before the Truth in Lending Law, the lender probably would have advertised this loan as a 10 percent interest loan, just like the lender for George's loan. In reality, are both of them paying the same interest rate?

Financial Fitness for Life: Bringing Home the Gold Student Workouts, ©National Council on Economic Education

Continued

They are certainly paying the same amount of interest, but they are not paying the same rate of interest. Why? In the first situation, the person receiving the loan has the full $1,200 for the entire year. In the second situation, part of the $110 a month is going toward the repayment of the loan. Sheila has less of the loan each month because of the monthly payments.

The Truth in Lending Law was established so that individuals shopping for credit could have a common basis for comparing loans. According to this law, the interest rate must be stated as an Annual Percentage Rate (APR), based on the declining balance of the loan. The Truth in Lending Law also requires that the full amount of finance charges (interest plus other charges) must be indicated to the consumer.

The formula for determining the APR for any loan is:

$$APR = \frac{2MI}{P(N + 1)}$$

M—Number of payments per year
(For monthly payments this is always 12)

I—Interest

P—Principal

N—Total number of payments

Let's figure out the APR for Sheila's loan by first looking at the interest that she pays.

$120 = $1,200 (principal) X .10 (interest rate) X 1 (number of years)

Now let's figure the annual percentage rate using the APR formula .

$$APR = \frac{2 \times 12 \times \$120}{1,200 \times 13} = \frac{2,880}{15,600} = 18.46\%$$

Notice that the APR for Sheila is much higher than the 10 percent that was probably quoted to her by the lender. If you use the formula for George's loan, you will see that it will come out to 10 percent APR since there was no declining balance on the loan. He always had $1,200 available on the loan.

Questions

Now let's figure some APRs. All these loans are paid back on a monthly basis.

1. Lisa Rosas borrows $5,000 at a 5 percent add-on rate for one year.

What is the finance charge?

What is the APR?

2. Brett Olson borrows $6,000 for three years at a 7 percent add-on rate.

What is the finance charge?

What is the APR?

3. What is the relationship of an APR for an add-on rate for a one-payment loan compared to an add-on for a monthly installment loan?

EXERCISE
15.1

Comparing Credit Cards

Americans love credit cards. Here are some statistics that show how widespread credit card use was in the United States in 1999.

- The average American household with at least one credit card carried a total credit card balance of $7,564. In 1990, the typical American household with at least one credit card had a balance of $2,985.

- Seventy-eight million of the 105 million households in the United States had at least one credit card.

- The average annual percentage rate on all bank credit cards was 17.11 percent.

- The revolving balance of credit card debt totaled $580 billion. That included $490 billion on bank credit cards and $90 billion on store credit cards.

- Americans charged more than one trillion dollars on their VISA, MasterCard, Discover, and American Express cards.

- There were 506 million VISA, MasterCard, Discover, and American Express cards in circulation in the United States. There were another 800 million debit and credit cards in circulation.

(These statistics were provided by CardWeb.com, a credit card research company. Its web site is **www.cardweb.com**. The statistics are for 1999.)

Shopping for a credit card can save you money. Not all credit cards are alike. Here are some ways in which they differ.

1. **The annual fee**. Some credit cards charge an annual fee, and some do not. The amount of the annual fee also can vary.

2. **Other fees.** Credit cards usually have stated fees for late or missed payments, going over your credit limit, or certain transactions such as cash advances.

3. **The annual percentage rate**. The APR can vary from card to card by several percentage points. Furthermore, some credit cards offer a low APR for the first few months and then increase it after three or six months.

4. **The grace period**. This is the amount of time a cardholder has to pay the credit card balance without paying interest. The longer the grace period, the more interest-free days the cardholder has. If the entire balance is paid within the grace period, no interest is due.

5. **The way interest is figured**. There are three methods of calculating credit card interest. These are:

   ✔ Average daily balance: The interest rate is calculated each day on the average of each day's balance for the billing cycle. This is the most frequently used method.

   ✔ Adjusted balance: The interest rate is calculated on the opening balance after subtracting the payments made during the month.

   ✔ Previous balance: Interest is calculated on the opening balance regardless of payments made during the month.

6. **The credit limit.** This is the maximum amount of money a cardholder can charge. A higher credit limit gives the cardholder flexibility but can also lead to credit card balances that are difficult to pay off.

Credit cards also differ in the types of services offered; this can be a reason to choose one card over another. Some of these services are:

✔ High or no credit limits.

✔ Rewards for the cardholder such as cash back, free gifts, frequent flyer airline miles, or a discount on a new car.

✔ The number of merchants who accept the card.

✔ Travel services such as covering the rental car insurance deductible, discounts on hotels, travel life insurance, or check-cashing privileges.

Question

1. **What characteristics should you look for if you want to save money on a credit card?**

Financial Fitness for Life: Bringing Home the Gold Student Workouts, ©National Council on Economic Education

Reading a Credit Card Statement

A credit card statement reveals a lot about what it costs to charge stuff and then pay interest on the loan. Let's see what information is found on a typical statement. Take a look at the credit card statement below:

Credit Is U
AMERICA'S CREDIT CARD COMPANY

Cardmember Name:
Tim Gray
1562 W. Wells Way
Lakeland, FL 33803

Credit Is U

Account Number:	000 000 0
Payment Due Date:	2-19-01
Minimum Payment:	.00
Total Amount Due:	1124.17
Amount Enclosed:	_____
Mail Payment to:	PO Box 00000000 Newark, DE 19716

Detach and mail this portion with your check or money order to the address above. Do not staple or fold.

Account Number	Billing Date	Payment Due Date	Days in Billing Period
000 000 0	01-25-01	02-19-01	32

Date	Reference Number	Description	Amount
1-14-01	01010101	CD Haven	22.30
1-21-01	02020202	Pizza, Etc.	8.33

Credit Line: $7,500   Credit Available: $6.336

Previous Balance	– Payments & Credits	+ Finance Charge	= New Balance	Minimum Payment
$1,072.30	.00	21.24	1,124.17	.00

The finance charge is determined by applying a periodic rate of	Which is an ANNUAL PERCENTAGE RATE of	To that part of the balance subject to finance charge of up to	Balance computation methods shown on reverse side
.05754% Daily	21.00%	Entire Balance	Average daily balance

Purchases, returns, and payments made just prior to billing date may not appear until next month's statement

Inquiries: Send inquiries (not payment) to : PO Box 222, Denver, CO 80202
Notice: See reverse side for important information.

Questions

1. How much did Tim Gray charge in the month of the statement?

2. Did Tim make a payment in the previous month? If so, how much was the payment?

3. What is the total credit available on this credit card?

4. How much of that credit was available at the time of this statement?

5. How does Tim's previous balance compare to the new balance shown on this statement?

6. Was Tim charged a finance charge this month? If so, what was the amount of the finance charge?

7. What is the annual percentage rate for credit on this account?

8. Looking at this statement, do you think Tim is handling his credit well? Why or why not? What would you recommend?

Using the Computer to Calculate Payments for a Loan

Computers can be very helpful in figuring out various aspects of a loan. In the following situation, you will be working with mortgages, which are big loans on houses. Payments are extended over many years, such as 15 or 30 years. Repayments on mortgages are generally made on a monthly basis.

The Internet has many mortgage calculators that can assist you in comparing the costs of various mortgages. If you cannot find a mortgage calculator, check with your teacher for help in securing one that you can use.

Let's analyze four different mortgages with different down payments, annual interest rates, and time periods. All of the homebuyers are purchasing a $125,000 house.

1. Sean and Amber Johnson pay 20 percent down and take out a $100,000 mortgage. It is a 30-year fixed-rate mortgage with an annual interest rate of 7 percent.

2. Alvin and Emily Jin qualify for a special mortgage program where the down payment is only 5 percent of the cost of the home. They take out a $118,850 mortgage. It is a 30-year fixed-rate mortgage with an annual interest rate of 7 percent.

3. Benny and Silvia Ramirez qualify for a special program that lowers their fixed annual interest rate to 6 percent. They make a 20 percent down payment and borrow $100,000 for 30 years.

4. Emily McGill knows that paying off a mortgage more quickly will save her money. She makes a down payment of 20 percent and borrows $100,000 at a fixed rate of 6.5 percent. Because she will pay off the mortgage in 15 years, her annual interest rate is lower than she would have paid for a 30-year mortgage.

Compare these four mortgages by completing the chart on the next page. Notice that the monthly payment and total payment (principal plus interest) are blank. You will fill these in using a mortgage calculator.

Using a mortgage calculator is easy. Just plug in the principal, annual interest rate, and term (in years) for each of the four mortgages. Check monthly payment amounts and total payments. Now use a mortgage calculator and fill in the rest of the chart. If your teacher does not give you a web site, try the Mortgage Bankers Association web site at **www.mortgagestogo.com/calculators.asp.**

96

Mortgage Chart

	Mortgage 1	Mortgage 2	Mortgage 3	Mortgage 4
Home price	$125,000	$125,000	$125,000	$125,000
Down payment %				
Down payment $				
Principal				
Annual interest rate				
Term				
Monthly payment				
Total interest				
Total payment (down payment, principal, and interest)				

Based on your chart, answer the following questions.

Questions

1. What happens to the monthly payment and total payment for a loan with a smaller down payment?

2. What happens to the monthly payment and total payment for a loan with a lower annual interest rate?

3. What happens to the monthly payment and total payment if the term of the mortgage is 15 years rather than 30 years?

4. What is the trade-off if you get a 15-year mortgage rather than a 30-year mortgage?

5. How can you reduce your cost of buying a home?

Getting the Best Deal on Your Auto Loan

Jill Winston shopped carefully for a new car. She found the model she wanted and negotiated a price of $18,000. She applied her old car's trade-in value to the down payment, which came to $6,000. Jill had to borrow $12,000 to buy the car.

Jill knew she should shop for credit just like she shopped for the car. She took the following steps:

Checked her credit rating. Jill made sure her credit rating was good and that there were no mistakes in her credit report.

Made comparisons. She checked rates at her bank and at one other bank. She also checked the rate the car dealer offered. She checked the rates at a finance company that advertised easy terms. Finally, she checked online for car loans offered at several web sites.

Compared loans for the same time period. Jill found an array of rates for different time periods. She decided that she should compare the rates for loans for the same time period. She chose a 3-year loan because longer loans mean higher finance charges. She also thought she might buy a new car in three years and wanted the loan paid off.

What Jill Found

The Last National Bank, where Jill has her checking account, offered her a loan with a 7.49 percent APR and a finance charge of $1,434.90. An online lending site offered Jill a loan with an 8.41 percent APR and a finance charge of $1,619.17. The car dealer offered her a loan with an APR of 9.5 percent and a finance charge of $1,838.23. Finally, the Friendly Finance Company offered her a loan with an APR of 13.95 percent and a finance charge of $2,754.25.

Now fill in the chart below to figure the best loan. Remember the total cost of the loan is the principal ($12,000) plus the finance charge. The monthly payment is the total cost of the loan divided by the number of months (36).

Kind of loan: _____   Principal: _____   Repayment period: _____

Name of Place	APR	Finance Charge	Total Cost	Monthly Payment
Last National Bank				
Online lending site				
Car dealer				
Friendly Finance Company				

Answer the following questions about Jill's loan:

Questions

1. Which loan is the best deal?

2. Which loan is the worst deal?

3. Jill took the best loan. How much extra did she pay because she financed her car instead of buying it for cash?

4. How much money did Jill save by taking the best deal rather than the worst deal?

EXERCISE 17.2

Shopping Online for an Auto Loan

Now it's time to shop online for a loan. Assume you want a new car loan; you will search for car loans and visit several web sites. Your new car costs $20,000. Your trade-in and down payment are $5,000. Therefore, the principal of the loan is $15,000. The repayment period is four years.

Kind of loan: _____   Principal: _____   Repayment period: _____

Web site	APR	Finance Charge	Total Cost
1.			
2.			
3.			
4.			

Questions

1. Which loan is the best deal?

2. Which loan is the worst deal?

3. How much money will you save by taking the best deal rather than the worst deal?

EXERCISE 17.3

Shopping in Your Community for an Auto Loan

Now it's time to shop for a loan at lending institutions in your community. Some possible places are banks, savings and loans, credit unions, and finance companies.

Again assume that you are buying a new car for $20,000. Your trade-in and down payment are $5,000, and the principal of the loan is $15,000. The repayment period is four years.

Kind of loan: _____ Principal: _____ Repayment period: _____

Name of Place	APR	Finance Charge	Total Cost
1.			
2.			
3.			
4.			

Questions

1. Which loan is the best deal?

2. Which loan is the worst deal?

3. How much money will you save by taking the best deal rather than the worst deal?

4. Did any lender offer a lower APR if you had a checking or savings account at that institution?

5. Would you get the best deal from a local lending institution or from an online source?

6. Name one advantage and one disadvantage of shopping for a loan in your local community compared to shopping for a loan on the Internet.

EXERCISE 18.1

Consumer Credit Protection

Credit problems are an important source of difficulty for young adults who are just getting started out of high school. Young adults sometimes make bad spending choices. They might live beyond their means. Excessive credit card debt is a common problem. So are high monthly car payments, high monthly rent payments, and the inability to save. For young couples, financial problems are often cited as the factors contributing to separation and divorce.

Financial problems, however, are not reserved for the young. People of all ages can face financial problems. An unexpected illness, loss of a job, divorce, or loss of child care are some of the factors that might tip a household into financial trouble.

Almost always, both sides benefit in a credit transaction. Borrowers are able to purchase something that may be of value today and perhaps in the future. Lenders are repaid the money that was loaned plus interest. If both sides consistently cheated and lied, the cost of credit would be very high and few could afford it. The vast majority of credit transactions are ones where all partners get what they want.

But the world is not a perfect place. Sometimes consumers of credit make mistakes or are dishonest with the credit provider. Sometimes credit providers make mistakes or are dishonest with the credit consumer.

Several state and federal laws are designed to protect credit consumers from dishonest business practices. State credit protection laws, of course, vary from state to state. You might want to contact your state bureau that handles such matters to learn more. The federal government has several laws regulating consumer credit. These include the *Truth in Lending Act*, *Fair Credit Reporting Act*, *Equal Credit Opportunity Act*, *Fair Credit Billing Act*, *Fair Debt Collection Practices Act,* and, most recently, the *Electronic Fund Transfer Act*.

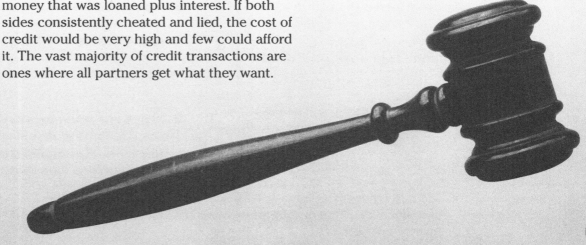

FEDERAL CONSUMER CREDIT PROTECTION

The **Truth in Lending Act** requires that creditors disclose the cost of credit in simple terms. The lender must state the percentage costs of borrowing in terms of the annual percentage rate (APR), which takes into account all the cost of financing. The lender must also disclose the total finance charges for the loan. The **Truth in Lending Act** also protects against unauthorized use of credit cards. If your card is lost or stolen, you are liable for no more than $50 of charges made by someone else. You cannot be held responsible for any charges after notifying the issuer. The **Truth in Lending Act** also requires that if a business advertises one credit feature (such as how many months to pay or the amount of the monthly payment), it must mention all other credit terms.

The **Fair Credit Reporting Act** governs the activities of credit bureaus and creditors. Among other things, the **Fair Credit Reporting Act** requires creditors to furnish accurate and complete information regarding your credit history. If you are refused credit, you have a right to see your credit report file from the bureau that submitted the negative information on which the decision was based. The **Fair Credit Reporting Act** requires credit bureaus to investigate if you disagree with information on your credit report. If your claim is valid, your report must be corrected. Finally, the **Fair Credit Reporting Act** requires that only people with a legitimate business purpose can obtain a copy of your credit report.

The **Equal Credit Opportunity Act** requires that all consumers will be given an equal chance to receive credit. The **Equal Credit Opportunity Act** states that it is illegal to discriminate against applicants on the basis of sex, marital status, race, national origin, religion, age, or because they receive public assistance income.

The **Fair Credit Billing Act** requires creditors to mail your bill at least 14 days before payment is due. It establishes procedures for correcting billing errors on your credit card accounts. This includes fraudulent charges on your credit card.

The **Electronic Fund Transfer Act** provides consumer protection to people who use ATM and debit cards. The act limits your liability when your card is lost or stolen. How quickly you report the loss determines the amount for which you are held responsible. If you report your ATM card lost or stolen within two days of discovering the loss or theft, your losses are limited to $50. If you wait up to 60 days, you are liable for up to $500. If you wait more than 60 days, you could lose all the money that was taken from your account.

The **Fair Debt Collection Practices Act** forbids collection agencies from using threats, harassment, or abuse to collect debts. This act does not apply to creditors who are collecting their own debts.

Financial Fitness for Life: Bringing Home the Gold Student Workouts, ©National Council on Economic Education

EXERCISE 18.1 Continued

Questions

1. What credit problems are common among young adults?

2. What are common causes of credit problems among other age groups?

3. What levels of government offer consumer credit protection?

4. Why do most credit transactions benefit both the borrower and the lender?

Questions (continued)

5. What act protects consumers from unauthorized use of credit cards?

6. What act forbids collection agencies from using harassment to collect debts?

7. What act requires creditors to bill you at least 14 days before payment is due?

8. What act protects credit consumers against discrimination on the basis of sex or race?

9. What act sets a process for consumers to correct inaccuracies in their credit report?

10. What act offers some protection when using a debit card?

Financial Fitness for Life: Bringing Home the Gold Student Workouts, ©National Council on Economic Education

Credible Credit Counselors

Part I **YOUR JOB**

You are a credit counselor. You specialize at explaining to your clients their rights under federal law and their responsibilities as borrowers. You offer your customers advice on possible actions they should take in regard to their credit problems.

After reading each client's case, answer the following questions:

Questions

1. According to federal law, what are the legal rights of your client?

2. Are your client's legal rights being violated?

3. Is your client being responsible or irresponsible?

4. What should your client do?

Part II **THE CLIENTS**

Client 1

I am 18 years old and I just started college. My parents gave me a debit card. I lost it. I didn't use it much. I didn't know that it was lost until my mother called and told me that she found all these outrageous charges on her statement. The card was used to charge over $5,000. Mom said that she contacted the card issuer the day she found the outrageous charges, which was about 3 weeks after I must have lost it.

Client 2

I am 23 years old and a recent graduate from a technical school and have my first office job. I have fallen behind in making my car payments. My bank has now contacted a collection agency to collect the loan. Now, I don't answer the telephone. The collection agency calls me every hour of the day and night. I am getting calls at work, and it is embarrassing to have other people see the messages left by the collection agency. Keeping this job is my best chance to get the money to start paying the loans but that will take a few weeks.

Client 3

I am 21 and have a new apartment. I am looking for a new sofa. I was reading newspaper ads to see what kinds of financial terms I could get. One full-page ad caught my attention. It said, "No money down, only $9.99 a month." I thought this sounded too good to be true, but the ad said nothing more about how much the sofa costs, how many monthly payments would have to be made, or the interest rate.

Client 4

I am 31 years old and recently separated from my spouse. I applied for a credit card in my own name. Today, I received a letter from the credit card company. It said, "We are sorry. Your application for credit has been denied." How could that be? I have always paid my bills on time. My former spouse sometimes had credit trouble but not me. The letter was no help at all.

Client 5

I am 22 years old. I reached into my pocket today and my wallet was gone. I don't know exactly when it disappeared. I could have lost it when I was in a crowded movie theater a couple of nights ago. I lost $75 in cash, my driver's license, and two credit cards. I am going to the Department of Motor Vehicles today to get a new driver's license. I will get around to calling the credit card people in a few days.

Client 6

We are a newly married couple. We are shopping for a car and a loan with which to buy it. The first lender we spoke to told us that the rate for the loan was only 7 percent. However, in addition to the interest charged on the loan, there was a loan fee of $200 to consider. Can they do that?

Legal Protection for Borrowers

Directions: Listed below are several problems. Place a check mark in the correct column indicating which federal law addresses the problem.

Federal Legislation ▶ Problem ▼	Truth in Lending Act	Fair Credit Reporting Act	Equal Credit Opportunity Act	Fair Credit Billing Act	Electronic Fund Transfer Act	Fair Debt Collection Practices Act
1. A collection agency is making harassing telephone calls about a collection.						
2. A creditor refuses to give you credit because you receive public assistance income.						
3. Your credit card is lost or stolen; you are liable for $50 of charges made by someone else.						
4. A creditor refuses to lend to you because you are African-American.						
5. A bank refuses to tell you why you were turned down for credit.						
6. You disagree with statements made in your credit report. A bank refuses to tell you why you were turned down for credit.						

Federal Legislation ▶ Problem ▼	Truth in Lending Act	Fair Credit Reporting Act	Equal Credit Opportunity Act	Fair Credit Billing Act	Electronic Fund Transfer Act	Fair Debt Collection Practices Act
7. You are liable for $50 on your debit card if a loss or theft is reported immediately.						
8. The first bill for your car payment arrives and you realize that you have only five days to pay it.						
9. A creditor tells you that the interest rate for vacation loans is only 7% per month.						

Scams and Schemes

Millions of credit transactions are completed each day. In the vast majority of cases, both sides benefit. But the world is not a perfect place. The credit industry, like any other industry, has a few people who operate on the edge. Some of these people are flat-out thieves. Others operate businesses that are completely legal but can place people who are already in financial trouble into a position from which it will be hard to recover.

Not all financial scams and schemes involve credit. Some deal with investments. They appeal to your desire to make a bundle of cash overnight. But, if it sounds too good to be true, it probably is.

Here are some of the more common scams and schemes.

1. WHAT IS IDENTITY THEFT?

Can you be electronically kidnapped? Yes. Scam artists get your name, Social Security number, credit card number, or some other piece of personal information. They use this information to open a new credit card account, using your name, date of birth, and Social Security number. When they use the credit card and don't pay the bills, the failure to pay is reported on your credit report. The scammers may call your credit card issuer and, pretending to be you, change the mailing address on your credit card account. Then they make charges on your account. Because your bills are being sent to a new address, you may not realize there's a problem. Scheme artists can do all sorts of other damage. They may open cellular phone service in your name. They might open a checking account in your name and write bad checks. Identity theft is illegal.

2. WHAT IS A LOAN SCAM?

An advertiser runs an ad offering a personal debt consolidation loan, taking all your credit payments and rolling them into one. Rarely is a company name or street address given. Instead, the "lender" has an 800 or 900 telephone number for you to call. When a consumer calls, the company representative asks only minimal information about the loan you want and about your financial history. He or she explains that the customer will be called back to indicate whether or not the loan was approved. All the loans, of course, are approved. The consumer is then instructed to send in a fee in return for the promised loan. The loan, of course, never arrives. A loan scam is illegal.

3. WHAT IS A CREDIT REPAIR SCHEME?

A company advertises that it can erase your bad credit history or remove bankruptcy from your credit records. The company requests that a fee be paid up-front for which the company promises to "repair" the consumer's credit report. However, there is little, if anything, such a business can do to "repair" a customer's poor credit record. There are no quick or easy ways to repair a poor credit history. A credit repair scheme is illegal.

110

4. WHAT IS A COLLEGE FINANCIAL AID SCAM?

A company advertises that millions of dollars in scholarships go unclaimed every year. The company promises that it will do the research to find a scholarship. The company requests that a fee be paid up-front, usually $200-$400. The company promises that if it can't find a $2,000 scholarship, it will return the fee. What will a college student get in return? Probably some scholarship information that is available at no cost to anyone who wishes to look. Guidance counselors and college financial aid officers are good sources of reliable scholarship information available at no charge to you. The scam is illegal.

5. WHAT IS A PYRAMID SCAM?

The key to a pyramid scam is that first participants receive payment for recruiting additional members. The problem with pyramid scams is that there are not enough potential members to keep pyramids growing steadily for even a few months. These plans often promise that if you sign up as a distributor of, say, telephone calling cards, you will receive commissions—not only on your sales but also on the sales of the people you recruit as distributors. Pyramid scams, however, can take several forms. They can be disguised as games, buying clubs, chain letters, mail order operations, or multi-level business opportunities. A pyramid scheme is illegal.

6. WHAT IS A PAYDAY LOAN?

A payday loan allows a person to get cash until payday with no credit background check. It is a legal loan and it can help some people in an emergency. An applicant for a payday loan typically provides paycheck stubs, savings account, and checking account numbers to the lender. The person receiving the loan writes a postdated check that is given to the lender. It is written for more money than the amount of the loan. The check is postdated so that it can be cashed later—generally two weeks after the loan was made. The check is then cashed by the lender after the date on the check. Typically, the interest rate (APR) is quite high. The APR may be 500 percent or higher. It is easy for people in financial trouble to fall behind in paying off a payday loan. They wind up taking out another loan and then another. Soon the finance and interest payments are more than the amount they borrowed.

7. WHAT IS RENT-TO-OWN?

Rent-to-own companies rent and sell appliances, furniture, and electronic products to consumers. Rent-to-own is a legal business. It allows consumers some advantages, such as returning an appliance or furniture after a short period of time. Typically, a consumer agrees to rent something for a short period—one week or a month. If the consumer rents the product for a specified period of time (often 18 months), the consumer will become the owner of the product either automatically or by making an additional payment. How might this business practice become a scheme? Purchasing merchandise from a rent-to-own company usually costs 2 to 5 times as much as purchasing the goods from a department store or appliance store. If the difference in the total payments and a fair price for the product were expressed as an interest rate, the rate could commonly be over 100%.

Continued

Match the Scam/Scheme to Its Definition

Directions: Match the name of the scam/scheme in the column on the left to its definitions on the next page.

Scam or Scheme	Definition
Rent-to-own	
Credit repair scheme	
College financial aid scam	
Pyramid schemes	
Payday loan	
Identity theft	
Loan scam	

A. A fraudulent company offers to erase a bad credit history or remove bankruptcy information from credit records. It collects an up-front fee and can do nothing to "repair" a customer's poor credit record.

B. A fraudulent company offers to find a student a scholarship. It collects an up-front fee and fails to provide the scholarship.

C. Scam artists get your name, Social Security number, credit card number, or some other piece of your personal information and use this information to open a new credit card account, cellular phone account, or checking account.

D. A fraudulent company offers a personal debt consolidation loan, collects an up-front fee, and never provides the loan.

E. A legal loan that allows a person to get cash until payday with no credit background check. Typically, the interest rate (APR) is quite high.

F. A fraudulent company in which the first participants receive payment for recruiting additional members.

G. A legal scheme offered by some businesses where the consumer pays a lot more money for appliances, furniture, and electronic products because of first renting the item and then buying it.

Name That Scam

Directions: Read the scam described in Column A and match it to one of the names of the scams listed to the left. Place the letter of the correct answer in Column B.

A. Identity theft

B. Loan scam

C. Credit repair scheme

D. College financial aid scam

E. Pyramid scheme

F. Payday loan

G. Rent-to-own

Column A "The Pitch"	Column B "The Scam"
1. Make big money on your home computer. Join our eel burger distribution network. Cash in on this new health food craze. E-mail your friends. They can be distributors too.	
2. Need cash today? Can't wait until you get paid? You can get $50 to $500 in 15 minutes. No credit checks!	
3. Tired of the broken-down CD player with lousy speakers? Want to step up to a new system but are short of cash? We can make it happen today!	
4. Here is the deal of a lifetime guaranteed to make you and your friends rich in weeks. Pay $100 to play Jack Pot. In weeks you will make hundreds more. Don't miss out. This is your chance!	
5. You receive an outrageous telephone call from the collection agency saying you have failed to pay a bill for nearly $20,000. You explain that the correct name was used but the billing address for the account was wrong. Soon you hear from a bank in another state that you are overdrawn by $5,000 in a checking account you didn't know you had.	
6. Credit problems? You need not suffer forever! Let us help. We can remove bankruptcies, liens, and bad loans from your credit file forever! Join our hundreds of satisfied customers.	
7. Over your head in debt? Bill collectors harassing you? Can't sleep? We can help. We can find credit for you. It's guaranteed! Call 1-800-123-4567.	
8. Every year, thousands of college scholarships go unclaimed. Are you skimping along simply because you don't have "connections"? We can help. We guarantee you that we will find you a $1,000, $2,000, or even $5,000 scholarship. All your money is returned if you are not satisfied!	

Get a Plan:
Get a Grip on Life
OVERVIEW

Do you know people who handle money carelessly? Lots of seemingly smart people are clueless on where they stand financially. There is Beverly, a professional woman, who calls the bank every two or three months to find out what the balance is in her checking account. She has never reconciled her checking account, so she never knows what her balance is. What Beverly still hasn't learned is that people at her bank don't know what Bev's real balance is either, because they don't know what checks Beverly has written in the last day or two. Only Beverly knows that. And then there is Ben. Ben actually believes that he can write checks as long as he has blank ones to be used. Ben has been heard to say, "Why would the bank give me blank checks if I'm not supposed to use them?"

You can avoid financial life in the Bev and Ben lane. You can get on the fast track to wealth by becoming good at managing your money. It starts with knowing some basic information and using some common sense and then taking action. We recommend three steps.

First, get a grip on your spending. How can you do that? Use the old-fashioned way. Set up a budget. Make a list of your income and expenses. Then subtract your expenses from your income. If you have any surplus cash, plan how you will use it. Do this each month. Maybe you will learn that now is the time to get started with a mutual fund or stock account.

Second, get to know the various services offered by financial institutions in your community. Checking accounts are perhaps the most common financial service people use, but there are many others including ATMs, direct deposits, savings accounts, credit cards, installment loans, student loans, retirement accounts, and stock accounts. While there are many types of financial institutions, the four most important ones are commercial banks, savings and loans, credit unions, and brokerage firms. Open an account now at one or more financial institutions. Start with checking and savings, but don't wait long to start other, more rewarding savings programs. Becoming wealthy is within your grasp. Starting to save when you are young is absolutely the best time.

Finally, you need to learn how to protect yourself against risk. All choices involve risk. But some risks are greater than others. Buying insurance is a common way to reduce risk. There are many kinds of insurance to consider including auto, health, renter's, homeowner's, life, and disability. The type and amount of insurance you will need will change as you get older and as the value of your assets increases.

The best thing regarding these three tips and others covered in these lessons is that none of this is overly difficult. It might take some work, but you can learn this stuff. Your efforts now can have a big payoff later.

Questions

1. What is a budget?

2. What are examples of financial institutions?

3. What is the point of buying insurance?

4. What are common forms of insurance?

5. When is the best time to get started on saving your first million bucks?

FAQs

ABOUT GET A PLAN: GET A GRIP ON LIFE

1. What is net worth?
Net worth is a measure of what you are worth financially. Net worth is the current value of your assets minus your liabilities.

2. What does it mean to "pay yourself first"?
Treat savings like it is a fixed expense—the same as paying your rent or car payment. Set your saving goal and arrange your income and spending so that you can reach it.

3. What are some common services offered by financial institutions such as banks, savings and loans, credit unions, and brokerage firms?
There are many financial services with which to become familiar. These include checking accounts, savings accounts, certificates of deposit, direct deposit, deposit insurance, credit cards, installment loans, home mortgages, home equity loans, student loans, small business loans, retirement accounts, and accounts for the purchase of stocks, bonds, and mutual funds.

4. Can you write checks as long as you have blank checks?
No. Here is how it works. You deposit money in your checking account to cover checks that you write. The checks that you write are subtracted from your checking account. If you write checks for more than the amount of funds in the account, negative consequences await. Your bank and most creditors charge high fees for overdrafts, which is when the requested payments from the account are more than what is in the account. When you write a check for money you don't have in the account, you risk ruining your credit rating. If you repeatedly write checks for more than what is in your account, you will be taken to court and could be put in jail.

5. How does insurance work?
The idea is to spread out the risk over several payers. A pool of people contribute money to buy insurance with the expectation that only a few will actually experience a loss that will need to be covered.

6. When is the best time to get started on your first million bucks?
Now!

Budgets Are Beautiful Call-In Show

RADIO HOST BUDGET BOB

Hello, financial health fans! Welcome to the nation's newest financial advice show, *Budgets Are Beautiful.* This is the radio call-in show that lets you, the radio listener, get the latest advice on how to manage your family finances. Today our topic is how to improve your skills at managing your family's finances. Our guest today is a successful family financial planner, Dr. Penny Saver. Dr. Saver has helped hundreds of families and has a Ph.D., M.A., and an S.U.V. Hello, Dr. Saver. Welcome to the show.

DR. SAVER

Hello Bob, and hello to all those people who are tuned in today. I am ready to take your questions.

BUDGET BOB

Here is our first caller: Connie from Connecticut. You're on the air, Connie.

Connie

Hi ,Dr. Saver. I am having a disagreement with my husband regarding the meaning of some financial vocabulary. He had heard someone on another call-in show talking about how to spend **disposable income.** My husband laughed and said that **all** our income is disposable. He said that we dispose of all our income by the end of every month. Sometimes we dispose of our income **before** the end of the month. I think he was joking, but could you tell me: What do financial planners mean when they talk about disposable income?

DR. SAVER

Actually, your husband was not too far off. Disposable income is the money that you have to spend or save as you wish after you pay your taxes, Social Security, and the other deductions that have been taken out of your gross pay. While disposable income can be used in many ways, most families have important financial obligations. Rent, car payments, and food bills add up quickly, so tough choices need to be made.

BUDGET BOB

That sounds kind of gloomy, Dr. Saver. Do you have any advice for Connie and her husband on how to get better use out of their disposable income?

DR. SAVER

Financial planners suggest that setting up and sticking to a family budget is the first step toward financial success. I advise families to start by setting a monthly budget. To do this, you make a list of your income and expenses. Under income, list all the money you anticipate earning for the month. For most people, most income will be what they earn from their jobs. Then list your expenses. Under expenses, write all the expenses you think you will have in the month, item by item. Common expenses are rent, car payment, insurance, groceries, and so forth. Then, subtract your expenses from your income. I hope that this is a positive number! If it is—if you have more income than expenses— then you have surplus cash that can be put to other uses. If, however, the number is negative, then you will need to cut your expenses, increase your income, or spend some of your savings to get through the month.

BUDGET BOB

Here is our next caller: Calvin from California. You're on the air, Cal.

Calvin

Hello Dr. Saver. Thanks for taking my call. My wife and I started to write a monthly budget and we learned right away that not all expenses are the same. Some seem to stay pretty much the same each month while others change. Do other people have this same situation? Can you comment on the different types of household expenses?

DR. SAVER

Great question! Families ordinarily have what we call fixed expenses and variable expenses. Fixed expenses are ones that are relatively constant each month. These are a family's definite obligations such as a house payment, rent payment, car payment, medical insurance, and fuel for the car. These expenses are hard to change in the short term, so we say they are "fixed." Variable expenses are ones that are likely to change in the short term. Telephone, groceries, medical bills not covered by insurance, entertainment, recreation, charge account purchases, and so forth are variable expenses. These are expenses over which you have more short-term control.

BUDGET BOB

Dr. Saver, I sometimes hear advisors say, "Pay yourself first." In other words, set money aside from your disposable income to put into your savings plan. How does this idea of "pay yourself first" fit into the family's expenses?

Continued

DR. SAVER

I tell my clients to include their savings goal in the fixed expenses part of their budget. I like this approach because it shows how important saving is to future individual and family financial health. Under the saving part of the budget, a family or individual could list funds saved for emergencies, as well as other cash set aside for long-term savings and investments.

BUDGET BOB

Here is our next caller, Minnie from Minnesota. You're on the air, Minnie.

Minnie

I just love this show, Dr. Saver. Here is my question. My sister Emily told me that she heard on television that people might have high incomes and still have a low net girth. What's all this about net girth? Is it true that people who have high incomes are also thin?

DR. SAVER

Minnie, I think that you misunderstood your sister Emily. I think that she was referring to the idea of net **worth**, not net **girth**. Let me explain. People can have high incomes and still not be wealthy. When we measure wealth, we are measuring net worth. Here is how to figure your net worth. Net worth is determined by two factors. First, list your assets and their value. Assets are what a person owns including the value of any savings, house, car, and personal possessions. Next, list your liabilities. Liabilities are the money you owe others such as a home mortgage, car loan, credit card debt, college loans, and so forth. If your assets are greater than your liabilities, then you have a positive net worth. If your liabilities are greater than your assets, then you have a negative net worth. Individuals can have a large income and, due to their liabilities, still have a negative net worth.

Minnie

Can I follow up on that last point? Do you mean to say that you can't tell whether a person is wealthy just by knowing where they live, what they drive, and where they travel?

DR. SAVER

That is exactly what I mean, Minnie. People who live in big homes, drive extravagant cars, and take around-the-world cruises probably have high incomes. That does not mean that they are wealthy. We measure wealth by calculating net worth. Many people of modest income have achieved a high net worth—many are millionaires—by living below their means.

BUDGET BOB

Well, Dr. Saver, that is all the time we have for today's show. Thank you for being with us.

DR. SAVER

You're welcome, Bob. Thanks for inviting me.

BUDGET BOB

Be sure to join us tomorrow when we will speak to Ms. Bonnie Bonds, another financial advisor. Bonnie's topic is "What Is Gross About Your Gross Income?" We hope you will tune in to the show tomorrow. We will be waiting for your call.

Questions

1. **What is disposable income?**

2. **What does Dr. Saver recommend as the three parts of a family budget?**

3. **What are fixed and variable expenses? Use examples to illustrate each.**

4. **What does this idea of "pay yourself first" mean?**

5. **What is net worth?**

Financial Fitness for Life: Bringing Home the Gold Student Workouts, ©National Council on Economic Education

John and Marcia: Monthly Spending Plan 1

John and Marcia are a young married couple. They have a two-year old child named Ashley and a goldfish named Shark. John manages a local shoe store. Marcia recently graduated from college and is a manager-trainee at a local bank. Their combined monthly income is $3,200. They want to have a successful marriage, and they want to be financially successful.

John and Marcia have enough income to provide an adequate lifestyle. Their apartment is comfortable but not lavish. They take care of themselves, Ashley, and Shark with sensible diets, exercise, and medical care. They view maintaining health, life, disability, and renter's insurance as essential. They pay for child care at Terrific Tots Day Care so that both of them can work. They keep up with all their financial commitments, such as making payments on Marcia's college loan. They regard saving for retirement as important. Like other individuals,

they are locked into their fixed expenses, but they have more flexibility with the variable expenses.

Marcia and John know that they want a second car. It is difficult to manage their complex schedules—work, day care, grocery shopping, and trips to the doctor—with only one car. They recently set a goal to save up enough money in one year for the down payment on a second car.

John and Marcia are regular savers. They practice the idea of "paying yourself first." They currently have $175 withheld from their paychecks to provide a fund for emergencies. They plan to have $400 taken out for the next year to make the down payment on the second car.

Listed below are the "before" and "after" fixed expenses. The only one which has changed is "savings withheld." Figure out where they can draw the additional money for savings from their variable expenses. Also, answer the questions on the next page.

Monthly Budget	Before	After
Total income (both spouses work)	$3,200	$3,200
Fixed Expenses		
Housing	600	600
Life and disability insurance	60	60
Renter's insurance	15	15
Automobile insurance	80	80
Student loan	100	100
Savings withheld	175	400
Federal and state taxes	320	320
Social Security	245	245
Pension fund withheld	65	65
Total fixed expenses	**$1,660**	**$1,885**

Financial Fitness for Life: Bringing Home the Gold Student Workouts, ©National Council on Economic Education

VARIABLE EXPENSES

Meals (home)	300	_____
Meals (away from home)	100	_____
Utilities	180	_____
Automobile fuel, maintenance	65	_____
Medical	60	_____
Child care	260	_____
Clothing	55	_____
Gifts and contributions	55	_____
Magazines and newspapers	40	_____
Home furnishings and appliances	40	_____
Personal care	55	_____
Entertainment	100	_____
Vacation	120	_____
Credit card	55	_____
Miscellaneous/personal	55	_____
Total variable expenses	**$1,540**	_____
Total expenses	**$3,200**	**$3,200**

Questions

1. What are some examples of John and Marcia's fixed expenses?

2. What are some examples of John and Marcia's variable expenses?

3. John and Marcia have decided to practice the "pay yourself first" approach to saving for a second car. How do they pay themselves first?

4. Examine the monthly spending plan above. What sacrifices do you think John and Marcia should make in their variable expenses to meet their goal?

5. What are the benefits and costs of your recommended decisions for John and Marcia?

123

John and Marcia: Monthly Spending Plan 2

One year later, John and Marcia are pleased with their financial decisions. They have been able to reduce their expenses to purchase the second car. They have enjoyed the convenience of owning a second car, their income has increased, and Marcia's college loan has been paid off. But new challenges have arrived. The car payment is greater than the college loan was. While having two cars has made life much better, the extra car has added to insurance and car expenses. Also, increased income means the couple pays more in taxes and Social Security.

Marcia and John know that to be financially successful they need to begin acquiring better assets. Owning a home is on the top of their personal and financial wish list. They recently set a goal to save up enough money in no less than four years for a down payment on a "starter home."

John and Marcia currently have $400 withheld from their paychecks for savings. They plan to have another $100 taken out for the next year to start their home down payment fund.

Listed below are the "before" and "after" fixed expenses. The only fixed expense that has changed is "savings withheld." Figure out where they can draw the additional money for savings from their variable expenses. Also, answer the questions on the next page.

Monthly Budget	Before	After
Total income (both spouses work)	$3,520	$3,520
Fixed Expenses		
Housing	600	600
Life and disability insurance	60	60
Renter's insurance	15	15
Automobile insurance	130	130
Car loan	200	200
Savings withheld	400	500
Federal and state taxes	350	350
Social Security	270	270
Pension fund withheld	70	70
Total fixed expenses	**$2,095**	**$2,195**

VARIABLE EXPENSES

Meals (home)	285	_____
Meals (away from home)	50	_____
Utilities	180	_____
Automobile fuel, maintenance	90	_____
Medical	55	_____
Child care	260	_____
Clothing	55	_____
Gifts and contributions	55	_____
Magazines and newspapers	15	_____
Home furnishings and appliances	40	_____
Personal care	55	_____
Entertainment	75	_____
Vacation	100	_____
Credit card	55	_____
Miscellaneous/personal	55	_____
Total variable expenses	**$1,425**	_____
Total expenses	**$3,520**	**$3,520**

Questions

1. What is John and Marcia's new financial goal?

2. Examine the monthly spending plan above. What sacrifices do you think John and Marcia should make in their variable expenses to meet their goal?

3. What are the benefits and costs of your recommended decisions for John and Marcia?

Financial Fitness for Life: Bringing Home the Gold Student Workouts, ©National Council on Economic Education

What Are Financial Institutions?

Financial institutions help people manage, protect, and increase their money. Individuals may use different types of financial institutions in different stages in their lives. While there are several different sorts of financial institutions to study, we will examine four:

- Commercial banks
- Savings and loan associations (S & Ls)
- Credit unions
- Brokerage firms

In the past, each type of financial institution offered specific and limited services. Banks took deposits in the form of checking accounts, savings accounts, and certificates of deposit and they granted credit to qualified individuals. Savings and loans offered savings accounts and home mortgages. Credit unions were a type of member-owned cooperative. Credit unions made low-interest loans available to their members. Brokerage firms were businesses that bought and sold stocks on an exchange, and offered other financial services.

Deregulation in the financial industry has blurred the lines between these institutions and increased competition among them. Deregulation means that laws were enacted to remove some of the restrictions (or regulations) that affected the industry. For example, savings and loans can offer many types of loans in addition to home mortgages as well as checking accounts. Many commercial banks can now sell stock.

Overview of Financial Services

DEPOSIT SERVICES

Types	Characteristics
Checking accounts	The convenience and safety of paying by check instead of cash.
Savings accounts and certificates of deposit (CDs)	Safe places to let your money grow.
Automated teller machines (ATMs)	Easy access to your money from multiple locations, 24 hours a day.
Direct deposits and automatic withdrawals	The ability to deposit money or pay bills automatically.
Deposit insurance	The guarantee that your deposits are insured by the federal government for up to $100,000 per depositor. Agencies which provide this insurance are FDIC (banks and S&Ls) or NCUA (credit unions).

126

CREDIT SERVICES

Types	Characteristics
Credit cards	The ability to access credit conveniently up to the amount of your approved credit limit.
Installment loans and credit lines	The opportunity to borrow for major items such as a new or used automobile, education, home improvement, and other personal or household items.
Mortgages	The opportunity to borrow for a home purchase.
Home equity loans	The ability to borrow against the equity in your home.
Student loans	The ability to borrow at below-market rates to pay for a college education.
Small business loans	The ability to borrow for the financial needs of a small business.

INVESTMENT SERVICES

Types	Characteristics
Retirement accounts (IRAs, SEPs, KEOGHs)	The ability to save money toward retirement on a tax-deferred basis.
Stocks, bonds, and mutual funds	The ability to invest in corporations and governments in order to meet your financial needs for the future.

Questions (2-5 continued on next page)

1. Name four common financial institutions.

Questions (continued)

2. How are financial institutions changing?

3. What are some of the common deposit services?

4. What are some of the common credit services?

5. What are some common investment services?

Checking Out Checking Accounts

Financial institutions offer many kinds of services. Perhaps the most widely used financial service is the checking account. A checking account allows you to deposit money into an account. You then can write checks or drafts to withdraw money from the account as you wish. This type of account is also called a demand account because you can demand or use the money in your account as you wish. Only the depositors can write checks on the account. Financial institutions usually charge a fee or require a minimum balance to maintain a checking account.

The checklist that follows provides an overview of steps involved in getting started with your first checking account.

Opening a checking account	• Take identification to the bank officer who handles new checking accounts. • Choose the type of checking account that best fits your needs. • Complete a signature card. • Make an opening deposit.
Choosing a checking account	There are three main types of checking accounts: • Special account: Service fees are charged at a low, flat rate with an additional fee for each check written. This account is often appropriate for a high school student. • Standard account: Set monthly fee with no check charge. May avoid a fee with a minimum balance. • Interest bearing account: Interest is paid if you maintain a minimum daily balance during the month.
Making a deposit	• Know the parts of a deposit slip. See the model in Illustration 21.1. • Write the date. • Write the amount of currency and coins to be deposited in the box marked "cash." • If checks are being deposited, write in the amount of each check. • Total the cash and check amounts. • Subtract any cash you wish to receive back. • Keep a copy of the deposit slip for your records. • Record the date and the amount of the deposit in your check register. Add the amount of the deposit to the balance.
Endorsing a check	• An endorsement is a signature on the back of a check instructing the bank on how the check may be cashed.

129

Endorsing a check *(continued)*	• A blank endorsement is simply your signature on the back of the check. This makes the check as good as cash to anybody who holds it. • A restrictive endorsement tags a check for a specific purpose, such as for deposit only to a checking or savings account. • A special endorsement allows you to transfer the check to another person. No one except the person named in the endorsement may cash or deposit the check.
Writing a check	• Know the parts of a check. See the completed check in Illustration 21.2. • Complete all the parts of the check including date, "pay to the order of" (payee), numeric amount, written amount, and signature line. If you wish, complete the memo line to indicate the purpose of the check. • Use a pen. • Write clearly. • Sign your name as it appears on the signature card. • When you make a mistake, write void on the check and keep the check for your records. • Be sure that you have enough money in your account to cover each check you write. • Record the number, date, payee, and amount of the check in your check register. Subtract the amount of the check from the balance.
Reconciling your checkbook	• Financial institutions send a monthly statement that summarizes the activity of your checking account including deposits, checks written, service charges, and any interest earned. • Compare your checkbook register to the monthly statement. Check off deposits and withdrawals. Record in the register any service charges or interest earned listed on the bank statement but not in the register. • Use the printed form sent by the financial institution with your statement to reconcile your checking account. • Write the ending balance as shown from the statement. • Add deposits to the ending balance that are listed in the register but not on the statement. • Subtract withdrawals listed in the register but not on the statement. • Note the adjusted balance; it should equal the checkbook register. • If the account does not balance, research possible explanations such as having missed checks that did not clear the account, fees charged, interest paid, calculation errors, or transposed numbers.
ATMs and debit cards	• Automated teller machines (ATMs) allow you to conveniently deposit, withdraw, or transfer funds, and verify your account balance. • ATMs use a PIN (personal identification number) to allow you to do a transaction. • A debit card is issued by many financial institutions. • A debit card allows you to have the amount of a purchase withdrawn directly and immediately from your checking account. • Be sure to keep receipts when you use your debit card, and record the transactions in your check register, including any additional changes.

Questions

1. What is a checking account?

2. Why do you suppose the signature card is important when you open a checking account?

3. What kind of a checking account is appropriate for most high school students?

4. What is a blank check endorsement for a check?

5. When should you void a check?

6. What is a debit card?

Financial Fitness for Life: Bringing Home the Gold Student Workouts, ©National Council on Economic Education

A Completed Deposit Ticket

Look at the sample deposit ticket as you read the procedures for filling one out.

1. Write the current date.

2. Write the amount of currency and coin to be deposited in the area for "cash."

3. If checks are being deposited, write the amount of each check separately in the area for checks.

4. Total the cash and checks and write that amount in the "total" box.

5. If you wish to receive cash back (usually when you are depositing only checks), write the amount in the "less cash received" box.

Sarah Jones
123 Luxury Lane
Richmondville, NC 27710

DEPOSIT TICKET

DATE _____ June 9 _____ 20 _02_

Bank of America

⑆0210000211⑈ 374

CASH	50	00
CHECKS	105	00
	3	00
	53	00
TOTAL FROM OTHER SIDE		
TOTAL	211	00
LESS CASH RECEIVED	50	00
TOTAL ITEMS **NET DEPOSIT**	161	00

BE SURE EACH ITEM IS PROPERLY ENDORSED

1·2/374
210

This deposit is accepted subject to verification, the provisions of the uniform commercial code and the rules and regulations of this financial organization Deposits may not be available for immediate withdrawal.

ILLUSTRATION 21.2

The Finer Points of Writing a Check

Look at the sample check as you read the procedures for filling one out.

1. Write the current date.

2. Write the name of the person or company you would like to pay. This person is called the payee.

3. Enter the amount of the check in numbers, including a decimal point and cents. Start the numbers as close to the dollar sign as possible.

4. Enter the amount of the check in words. Start writing from the far left side of the line. Follow the dollar amount by the word *and*, then write the cents amount as a fraction, over 100. (If there are no cents, use 00.) Draw a line from the end of your writing to the end of the line so there is no additional room to insert words or numbers.

5. Sign your check the same way you signed the signature card when you opened your account.

6. Write the purpose of the check. You may also use this space to write the account or invoice number of the bill you are paying.

Sarah Jones
123 Luxury Lane
Richmondville, NC 27710

0993

Date *April 28, 2001*   66-19/530 NC
73

$ 100.35

Pay to the order of   *Sylvia Rodriguez*

One Hundred and 35/100 _____ Dollars

Security features
are included.
Details on back.

Bank of America.

Sarah Jones   MP

For   *Used Furniture*

⑉053000196⑉ 00068794 1443⑉ 0993

Keeping a Checking Account

Instructions: Suppose that you have a checking account. Imagine that you are writing checks to businesses listed below and depositing money in the checking account. Complete the checks and the deposit tickets correctly and keep a record of each transaction in the check register.

March 1	Opened account with $250 deposit.
March 7	Paid $30 to CD Sales to buy some CDs which were on sale.
March 8	Paid $50 for sweater to A. J. Vitullo Company.
March 10	Paid $45.10 to the Acme Bicycle Shop for repairs to bicycle.
March 12	Paid Happy Pets Store $10.00 for pet supplies.
March 14	Deposited $50 gift money into account.
March 16	Paid $16 to Lawson High School for two tickets to area basketball game.
March 18	Took $50 out of account for spending money.

John Q. Public
123 Money Lane
Richmondville, NC 27710

DEPOSIT TICKET

DATE _____ 20 _____

_____

Bank of America.

CASH

CHECKS

TOTAL FROM OTHER SIDE

TOTAL

LESS CASH RECEIVED

TOTAL ITEMS NET DEPOSIT

BE SURE EACH ITEM IS PROPERLY ENDORSED

1-2/374
210

This deposit is accepted subject to verification, the provisions of the uniform commercial code and the rules and regulations of this financial organization. Deposits may not be available for immediate withdrawal.

⑈021000021⑈ 374

134

John Q. Public
123 Money Lane
Richmondville, NC 27710

DEPOSIT TICKET

DATE _____ 20____

Bank of America.

⑈0 2ⵏ0000 2ⵏ⁝ ⵏ74

CASH	
C H E C K S	
TOTAL FROM OTHER SIDE	
TOTAL	
LESS CASH RECEIVED	
TOTAL ITEMS NET DEPOSIT	

BE SURE EACH ITEM IS PROPERLY ENDORSED

1-2/374
210

This deposit is accepted subject to verification, the provisions of the uniform commercial code and the rules and regulations of this financial organization. Deposits may not be available for immediate withdrawal.

PLEASE BE SURE TO DEDUCT CHARGES THAT AFFECT YOUR ACCOUNT

CHECK #	DATE	TRANSACTION DESCRIPTION	WITHDRAWAL/ SUBTRACTIONS	✓ T	FEE IF ANY	DEPOSIT/ ADDITIONS	BALANCE

John Q. Public
123 Money Lane
Richmondville, NC 27710

0994

Date _____

66-19/530 NC
73

Pay to the
order of _____ $ [   ]

Dollars

Security features
are included.
Details on back.

Bank of America.

For _____   _____ MP

⑈053000196⑈ 000687941443⑈ 0994

John Q. Public
123 Money Lane
Richmondville, NC 27710

0995

Date _____

66-19/530 NC
73

Pay to the
order of _____ $ [   ]

Dollars

Security features
are included.
Details on back.

Bank of America.

For _____   _____ MP

⑈053000196⑈ 000687941443⑈ 0995

John Q. Public
123 Money Lane
Richmondville, NC 27710

0996

Date _____

66-19/530 NC
73

Pay to the
order of _____ $ [   ]

Dollars

Security features
are included.
Details on back.

Bank of America.

For _____   _____ MP

⑈053000196⑈ 000687941443⑈ 0996

John Q. Public
123 Money Lane
Richmondville, NC 27710

0997

Date _____ 66-19/530 NC
73

Pay to the
order of _____ $ _____

_____ Dollars 🔒 Security features
are included.
Details on back.

Bank of America.

For _____   _____ MP

⑈053000196⑈ 0006879411443⑈ 0997

John Q. Public
123 Money Lane
Richmondville, NC 27710

0998

Date _____ 66-19/530 NC
73

Pay to the
order of _____ $ _____

_____ Dollars 🔒 Security features
are included.
Details on back.

Bank of America.

For _____   _____ MP

⑈053000196⑈ 0006879411443⑈ 0998

John Q. Public
123 Money Lane
Richmondville, NC 27710

0999

Date _____ 66-19/530 NC
73

Pay to the
order of _____ $ _____

_____ Dollars 🔒 Security features
are included.
Details on back.

Bank of America.

For _____   _____ MP

⑈053000196⑈ 0006879411443⑈ 0999

137

Financial Services Survey

FACTS ABOUT FINANCIAL INSTITUTIONS

Name of financial institution _____

Address _____

Total number of locations _____   Hours/days _____

Membership or other qualifications required to do business _____

Type of institution (check one)
❑ Bank
❑ Brokerage firm
❑ Credit union
❑ Savings & loan association

Survey conducted (check one)
❑ By phone
❑ In person
❑ Other _____

Check all financial services that this institution offers:
Deposit services
❑ Checking accounts
❑ Savings accounts
❑ Certificates of deposit (CDs)
❑ Direct deposit and automatic withdrawal
❑ Deposit insurance (such as FDIC)
❑ Automated teller machines (ATMs)

Credit services
❑ Credit cards
❑ Installment loans
❑ Lines of credit
❑ Mortgages
❑ Home equity loans
❑ Student loans
❑ Small business loans

Investment services
❑ Retirement accounts (IRAs, SEPs, KEOGHs)
❑ Stocks and bonds
❑ Mutual funds

138

EXERCISE 22.1

Choices and Risks

All choices involve risk. Let's consider driving a car. Everyone knows that there is always a risk of having an accident. You could cause an accident yourself or another driver could cause an accident that involves you. How can you reduce the risk of having an accident when driving? You have three choices. First, you can choose to stop driving. Ride the bus, ride a bike, or walk. Even though you are not required to drive, the no-driving alternative may seem extreme to you. Let's examine the remaining choices.

Second, you can become a safer driver. Take a course in defensive driving. Study the state road-safety manual. Pay attention in driver's education. Avoid driving during rush hours on dangerous roads and late at night. Third, you can purchase auto insurance. You can purchase insurance to protect you from financial loss for car repairs, medical costs, or lawsuits that result from an accident. You may still have a wreck, but the consequences will not be as bad as they would have been if you did not have insurance.

Your choices about driving are similar to many others. Usually your best way of reducing risk is to take actions yourself to reduce risks. For example, to reduce health problems, eat right, get plenty of exercise, get enough sleep, avoid drugs, and so forth. Buying health insurance is another way to reduce health-care cost risks. To reduce the chances of theft, install good locks, stop mail and newspaper deliveries when you are away, and keep areas around your house or apartment well lit. Buying home-

owner's or renter's insurance is another way to reduce the risk of financial loss from theft.

The purpose of insurance is to spread out risks over many people. Let's consider an example. Imagine that the student council in a high school of 1,000 students wants to offer all students insurance against the theft of personal possessions from school lockers. The student council has decided to establish a locker insurance company. Suppose that students in this school have an average of $50 worth of personal stuff in each locker. Suppose further that an average of 10 in every 1,000 lockers are broken into each year. In a typical year, students in the school lose a total of $500 ($50 of stuff x 10 locker break-ins) in locker theft. If all 1,000 students wish to buy insurance, it would cost:

$$\frac{\$500 \text{ loss}}{1000 \text{ students}} = \$.50 \text{ charge for each student for locker insurance}$$

If every student bought $.50 worth of locker insurance, they would be covered from financial damage due to locker break-ins. This is fundamentally how insurance companies work. Insurance companies charge a fee (a premium) paid by customers to provide protection against certain types of losses. The fee or premium would not only cover the losses but also the costs of operating the business and a profit.

Table 22.1 shows types of insurance you can buy for different types of risk. Study the table and you will be able to answer the questions at the end.

Types of Insurance

Type of Insurance	Purpose	Examples of Coverage
AUTO	Provides financial protection from losses due to an auto accident or other damage to a car.	COLLISION: Provides for the repair or replacement of the policy owner's car damaged in an accident. LIABILITY: Covers the cost of property damage or injuries to others caused by the policy owner. COMPREHENSIVE: Covers the cost of damage to an auto as a result of fire, theft, or storms.
HEALTH	Provides payment for certain health-care costs.	BASIC HEALTH: Covers office visits, laboratory, hospital costs and routine care. MAJOR MEDICAL: Protects against large bills from catastrophic illness or injury. DENTAL AND VISION: Covers some cost of routine exams and specific services.
RENTER'S	Provides financial protection in case of loss of personal possessions in a rental unit.	Reimburses policy owner for loss of possessions in a rental unit due to fire, theft, water damage, etc.
HOMEOWNER'S	Protects against financial loss from damage to your home or its contents, as well as injury to others on the property.	PHYSICAL DAMAGE: Reimburses for fire or water damage to house or other structures on the property. LOSS OR THEFT: Reimburses for personal property damaged or stolen. LIABILITY: Protects against loss from a lawsuit for injuries to invited or uninvited guests.
LIFE	Provides financial protection to dependents of policy owner when policy owner dies.	TERM LIFE: Offers protection for a specified period of time. WHOLE LIFE: Offers protection that remains in effect during the lifetime of the insured and acquires a cash value.
DISABILITY	Provides income over a specified period when a person is ill or unable to work.	Policy owner selects a replacement income for lost wages if an illness or accident prevents the person from working. Disability income is paid for a specified time after a waiting period.

Questions

1. All choices involve risks. Name two ways to reduce risks.

2. How does insurance work?

3. What is a premium?

4. What does each type of insurance provide?

- **Auto:**

- **Health**

- **Renter's:**

- **Homeowner's:**

- **Life:**

- **Disability:**

5. In the case of auto insurance, what is the difference between collision and liability coverage?

6. In the case of health insurance, what is the difference between basic health and major medical coverage?

Financial Fitness for Life: Bringing Home the Gold Student Workouts, ©National Council on Economic Education

The Big Risk

You have just graduated from high school or college, and you are single. You own a number of assets that you are thinking of insuring, including an automobile, inherited jewelry, a rare coin set, and the contents of your rented apartment.

Your employer provides a health insurance plan you can purchase. Examine the cost and the risk of each of the things you would like to insure below, and circle them. Do not spend more than $2,600; you may spend less. Indicate your choices below.

Renter's Insurance (theft, fire, acts of nature)		Jewelry Insurance		Automobile Insurance (collision, comprehensive, liability)	
Premium:	$100/year	Premium:	$45/year	Premium:	$1200/year
Loss:	$2,800	Loss:	$3,400	Loss:	$4,600
Risk:	1 in 12	Risk:	1 in 12	Risk:	8 in 12
Card:	9	Card:	7	Card:	5 - 12
Deductible:	$250	Deductible:	None	Deductible:	$250

Health Insurance (doctor visits, surgery)		Life Insurance (death)		Rare Coin Insurance (loss due to theft)	
Premium:	$650/year	Premium:	$300/year	Premium:	$170/year
Loss:	$1,200	Loss:	$100,000	Loss:	$1,000
Risk:	10 in 12	Risk:	*below* 1 in 12	Risk:	1 in 12
Card:	2 - 12	Card:	Must draw two 12s in a row	Card:	4
Deductible:	$10 co-payment	Deductible:	None	Deductible:	None
(Assuming 2 visits per year)					

Disability Insurance (long-term injury, illness)		My choices	
		Type of insurance	**Premium**
Premium:	$600/year		
Loss:	$14,400		
Risk:	7 in 12		
Card:	6 - 12		
Deductible:	None		

Adding Up Insurance

Card chosen	Year	Annual Premiums of Insurance Coverages You Chose	Losses Due to Unexpected Events When Insured (Deductibles, Co-pays)	Losses Due to Unexpected Events When Uninsured	Total Dollar Costs
1	2	3	4	5	6
6	EXAMPLE 1	0	0	$20,200	$20,200
6	EXAMPLE 2	$1,800 ($1,200 car insurance + $600 disability insurance)	$250 (Automobile Deductible) $0 (Disability)	$1,200 (Health)	$3,250
	1.				
	2.				
	3.				
	4.				
	5.				

TOTAL: _____

Questions for Discussion

1. How much were your losses over the period of the simulation?

2. What were the consequences of the insurance choices you made?

NOTES